DO EPIC SHIT

The Power of Showing Up

VICTORIA PORTER CRAMER

Also by Victoria Porter Cramer

Living Life Loudly – How Will You Face Your Speed Bump?

Copyright 2022 by Victoria Porter Cramer

All rights reserved. Except as permitted under the U.S. Copyright Act of 1976, no part of this publication may be reproduced, distributed, or transmitted in any form or by any means, or stored in a database or retrieval system, without the prior written permission of the publisher.

DISCLAIMER

This book contains the opinions and ideas of its author. It is intended to provide helpful and informative material. It is sold with the understanding that the author is not engaged in rendering medical, health, or any other kind of personal professional services in the book. The reader should consult his or her medical, health, or other competent professional before adopting any of the suggestions in this book or drawing inferences from it.

The author specifically disclaims all responsibility for any liability, loss or risk, personal or otherwise, which is incurred as a consequence directly or indirectly, of the use and application of any of the contents of this book.

This book is dedicated to my incredible family. My husband Mike is my best friend and most epic partner in life. My children Parker and Ryan challenge every fiber of my being and inspire me every day. I am honored to be in all of their lives today and for as long as is possible.

To Parker and Ryan: You are going to change the world. When you face your own challenges and pains, please remember you are stronger than you know, because a piece of me is inside of you. You are wired to handle hard things.

Parker, keep lighting up the world one person at a time and work hard to wake up seeing sunrises. Dance hard and laugh harder. Remind Ryan to not be too serious and keep her laughing and dancing. Never stop exploring and being creative. If you forget who you are then be a child again and name a dragon for anyone who needs one. Your mystical world makes my heart so full. I have Firefly the dragon because of you. Thank you.

Ryan, always show up no matter how nervous you are, because you will not regret it when you show up and if you do not, then you'll regret that you carried too much fear in your soul. Just remember, you wake up with remarkable energy and a smile that is so contagious and if you share it with others, they'll respond with gratitude and kindness. Remind Parker to keep practicing at anything she wants to be good at and be there to pick up her messes from time to time. Dang, you shine bright and excel at everything you put your heart into, so keep working hard, you've got this!

Mike, you are the only man I have truly ever loved. You have made me a better human. Never stop laughing, learning, and loving. Do everything that makes you nervous and lights your soul on fire. I'm pretty sure we can level up the shark scuba dives or the places we've snow skied. Our adventure-o-meter is something magical.

I also want to honor each and every cancer warrior because I see you and I know just how hard it is to be a warrior. For those who have fought and lost and for those who fight every day, I send you my love. I also thank the doctors and scientists working to rid this world of cancer or at least create awareness for how we can keep it from winning.

I also want to tell the "fish in my fish bowl" how much you mean to me. You know who you are and I just want to say thank you for swimming with us. We are a colorful bunch, aren't we?! You are my ride or die friends and family and I am sure grateful you let me be slow. ☺

HIGH FIVES FOR DO EPIC SHIT

"When I met Victoria at a 24-hour mountain bike race, I knew she was fucking awesome! The woman has done more races while on chemo than off and her approach to life is admirable. Enjoy her wit and be prepared to be inspired."

- Lance Armstrong

"This book captured me. I felt uplifted by the humor and inspired by Victoria's raw vulnerability. Experience her epic battle in this captivating page-turner. You will at a minimum be inspired - but also be prepared to reflect and make changes in your own life's adventure - I did!"

-Sarah Hiza, VP/GM Lockheed Martin Missile Defense Systems

CONTENTS

FORWARD

Do Epic Shit. The Power of Showing Up.

"No one gets off a comfy couch"
– Doctor East Haradin Phillips

The universe often makes your "couch" uncomfortable so that you will finally make the changes that will lead to your growth and happiness. I don't think I was ready for my couch to be uncomfortable, but the universe knew I could handle being tested.

Some of you walked beside me on my first battle with cancer, some met me after my battle, and others have read my first book "Living Life Loudly – How Will You Face Your Speed Bump?". Whether this is your first introduction to me or you've been here all along, I'd recommend you strap on your seatbelts, open your mind, and open your heart to experience a warrior's mindset.

As American literature and human experience expert Joseph Campbell once said, **"Your sacred place is where you can find yourself over and over again"** ...although I prefer my adaptation of this which is "Your scared place is where you find yourself over and over again".

So, when we last sat down together, I had just fought the fight to beat an aggressive form of breast cancer for the first time. After major surgeries and a year and a half of chemotherapy, I was working to negotiate some collateral damage. I was trying to figure out if I needed blood pressure medication, if I was ever going to stop getting bronchitis, and if my mind was going to start acting like the warrior chick's mind I had once known. I was filled with fear, because every CT scan every quarter would turn up "something to keep an eye on" for the next set of scans. I didn't want to live in fear and I was struggling to find my confidence. When you battle cancer, you hate chemo but you start to wonder if it's keeping you alive (while slowly killing you at the same time ha ha…it's an epic battle in your brain). It took about one-year post treatment, a clean Petscan, great blood work, and awesome blood pressures to stand proud and know that I was a survivor.

The emotional trauma was something else entirely. I lost all confidence in myself. My brain and my body seemed foreign and awkward. I will not get graphic but the scars on the outside paled in comparison to the scars on the inside. Looking in the mirror took a long time. I decided to cover up the scars with elaborate tattoos which did help me to feel pretty again. It was a hard bumpy road but I was healing.

My daughters had grown from toddlers to preschoolers'. They are twins who have lived their entire lives, not realizing it, but watching me fight every day to be here with them. To them, I just have a lot of doctor visits, and looking at some pictures they laugh and say my head was bald like theirs. I like that (until recently) they haven't known anything other than that they are on a cover of a book. They sure like to autograph it. It's pretty cute. I'm grateful, because fighting breast cancer a second time was an even longer journey with a lot of complexity, and the girls were still fairly oblivious to the battle that had to be fought. What you'll find out as we go along is that pretty quickly, I ended up fighting for a third time as well. Fighting and curating an epic life of happiness is all I really know. It's all my family knows. I think we are much better for it.

It is 2022. My daughters have just turned 8. I am 50 years old and have been fighting cancer for 8 years. If you're reading this then you too have survived COVID (which I likely will never have to explain) but I certainly will talk about in this book. You are a warrior and you may not even realize it. I am a warrior. I am resilient. I have the tools to survive epic battles in this lifetime, which I am going to share with you so you too can stand proud knowing you are a warrior. You will also be armed with how to do epic shit. You will come to realize that when I say "do epic shit", I do not mean that you are skydiving or traveling around the world, although those things are most certainly epic. What you'll come to realize is that it means doing things against the grain and curating a truly joyful life every single day.

A girlfriend of mine said, "We are not all in the same boat; we are in the same storm. In this storm, some have yachts, some have canoes, and some are drowning." This couldn't be more accurate. No matter what you've been given to weather the storm, we must all show compassion and help each other with the tools to thrive.

So, let's talk about that small timeframe in life when I didn't realize cancer was once again growing inside of me.

I had gotten even more competitive and strong in mountain biking while continuing to live life loudly.

What does it mean to live life loudly? Well, it means you choose joy and choose happiness deliberately. To live life loudly means to choose intentionally to master the exploration of happiness and to strip away the incrementalities in life, discovering things you can do to make every single day truly impactful.

Once in a coffee shop in a sweet little town called Pagosa Springs, CO, I found a journal that called to me, because it was leather and it had good quality heft to the paper. On the front of this journal is a quote that describes what it means to me to live life loudly:

"This is the beginning of a new day. You have been given this day to use as you will. You can waste it or use it for good.

What you do today is important because you are exchanging a day of your life for it. When tomorrow comes, this day will be gone forever. In its place is something that you left behind. Let it be something good."

Maybe an example would help? If you know you have only so many awake hours in a day, perhaps instead of folding that laundry, you decide to go for a walk with a neighbor or you take your kids for a sunrise coffee date. I know not every day can be a "skip the laundry" day but if you look at all of the opportunities in a day, could you pack in or infuse a lot more inspiration, kindness, connectedness, and happiness in a day? To me, living life loudly also means pushing my boundaries, doing the things that scare me, that make me squirm—doing them anyway. Some might think me an adrenaline junkie, but that's really not the case. I'm the girl excited to scuba dive with sharks, write a book (which for many is a scary endeavor and certainly has always been for me), snow ski on mountains I've never been to around the world, or skydive out of a perfectly rickety old airplane that looks like it's been duct taped together.

I guess living life loudly means different things to different people but the common factor is that whatever it is - it makes you squirm. So - if it makes you squirm, then you're probably making an epic day and doing exactly what I'm describing! I'd probably argue that even the absence of squirming, if you're traditionally used to working at a brilliantly fast pace, might be your version of living live loudly. A few friends have pointed out that when I enjoy a rare, unplanned, no-agenda day, I'm also living life loudly (Ha! —no agenda makes me squirm). It's a simplification project or a happiness barometer.

You're probably wondering what in the world any of this has to do with being a warrior or being epic. I will share with you that being a warrior is about having an extra special mindset. It is tied to having the ability to live life loudly and boldly on your own terms.

You will find that there is one thing that a warrior does differently. It is the difference between the person who accomplishes a New Year's resolution and one who does not. It is the difference between a winning athlete and one who is missing the mark. We will get there.

We all know people who are resilient. I now know that I am. I am actually grateful for the opportunities for learning each successive bout with cancer has provided. I am grateful to have been given the opportunity to fight cancer three times so that I could fully elevate my level of gratitude for the learning experiences that have been given to me. You see, to be resilient does not mean that you have to be happy all the time. It means that when you get through a spin cycle in life that you recover through those dark emotions faster than most.

There are some 'givens' for all humans. You will experience dark emotions like anger, sadness, anxiety, or fear. In fact, more research over the years has been dedicated to these emotions than to happiness, joy, or excitement. However, what we have learned is that dark emotions can be conquered. Those who conquer them most effectively are the ones who 'warrior through life'. The ones who are truly resilient. We will explore more ways to create that warrior mentality and face those emotions in a healthy and resilient way. Let's face it, you will get bucked off your horse and you must use that pain and discomfort to get you back on that horse stronger than ever.

One of the core questions I have asked myself is why does happiness matter? Aren't the strongest most powerful warriors emotionally void? Wouldn't it be better for my warrior mentality to just put up a wall and force out emotions or block them?

After my first battle with cancer, I realized that I was being strong for everyone around me because they needed me to be. I might have needed me to be as well. So, to protect myself from disappointment or fear, I would say I was "holding my breath" metaphorically. When "it" was all over, I floundered for quite a few months trying to figure out why I was feeling sad and scared. It was because I finally could let my breath out, but I had been holding it for so long and suppressing those emotions that breathing again paralyzed me for a moment.

When I was struck with battle #2, I asked my support network; my team; if they were willing to be along with me for this next phase of my journey and if they were, then what did they need from me this time that perhaps they did not get last time. The answer was a yes AND we need for you to share your feelings with us. Do not shield us from the raw emotions and do not suppress them. Sharing my feelings allowed my team to see a vulnerable side and together we faced the dark emotions and helped me get to the ones I was most known for; humor, tenacity, grace, and happiness.

I will share more about what I learned and experienced, however, the answer to the question, "am I a warrior?" became clear when a friend of mine kept calling me one. He said warriors "just show up". What he meant is that a large percentage of people choose to sit on the sidelines in life due to fear, anxiety, sadness, or anger. True warriors do not let those emotions keep them from experiences in life even if life is very hard. He asked me to take note that I am a warrior not only for showing up to every step of my own journey but also because I inspire others. I help all of those around me "to show up" to things in life that are so much easier to do than chemo or radiation or surgery. People who might not have wanted to get up to exercise on a given day or who did not want to go to a routine doctor's visit or even to the grocery store, had to think about my not wanting to go to radiation but showing up anyway every day for 7 weeks. It causes one to realize, you too can show up to that meeting or that doctor's appointment or workout to get your butt kicked.

So, the answer was clear. Choose to be happy. It is not a weakness. It is a warrior's trait. It is what fueled me on my first battle and it was going to be the fuel for my next battles.

Well, shall we get on with it? I think it's time to dive into the story of this warrior and for you to see how elevating gratitude, incorporating deliberate action, and exercising can lead to the highest currency – happiness.

It has often been said that I should come with a warning label, because I am raw and I curse like a sailor. So, this is your warning. You will need to strap on your seatbelt and be prepared to cringe from time to time, but once you see past the sarcasm and a few curse words, I think you'll see the warrior in me is also the warrior in you. (Ok, I will try to keep curse words to a minimum but if you see one just know it is raw and intense and not meant to be offensive).

Additionally, while I have been writing this book, the entire world has experienced the speed bump of a lifetime. This one literally affects every human on the planet. It has been what nightmares and horror movies are made of and it became real.

Covid 19 is a real virus that literally took over the world. As far as plagues go, it is ranked as one of the top 10 deadliest but in comparison to other plagues not nearly as horrific, because this one didn't start attacking children until much later and very few children have died from it. However, its economic impacts are felt by every human on the planet. Even if you did not have the virus, you may have had someone close to you die from it, you may have been laid off from your job because of it, you may have been forced to isolate because of it with little human contact for upwards of a year. Your children would have been forced out of schools and into online learning (which the majority of the population did not have internet access or had to quit jobs to support their children's learning). In my first book I describe these moments that take the wind out of you as speed bumps. Well, this one was a brutal speed bump. Of course, I would never wish for a pandemic to force everyone off of comfy couches but in this case, it brought about innovations, pioneers emerged, and tested our resilience. It has, unfortunately, also created intense depression, anxiety, and anger. No matter which emotion you resonate with most, it's time to learn or to teach; it's time to thrive and help others to see their path forward. We all have a role in this rebuild effort.

If you did not notice, there is a place in the back of this book to journal along the way. Or do what I have always done and take notes in the borders of the book. Just you do you.

Additionally, to know me is to know I enjoy coffee shops. I love having coffee chats and coffee shop dialogue. So, think of this as your sit-down chat with me. The way I write is also the way I talk. You should hear my voice and sometimes my unique approach coming through. If you do not know me, that is ok, you will hear a voice and hopefully it makes for a fun chat with your favorite cup of whatever you enjoy.

CHAPTER 1 – BLINDSIDED AGAIN

"For every minute you remain angry, you lose sixty seconds of happiness" – anonymous

Ya seriously WHAT THE HECK? How am I doing this again? So not right, but shit, I did create a perfect environment for those little jack ass cancer cells to grow…let's see, I like sugar, I like alcohol, I love biking and I keep my body totally inflamed from exercise and highly likely from gluten intolerances or maybe dairy or both. I gave it the fuel to grow with glucose and I gave it the inflammation it loves for a super comfy home. I may be only 130 pounds at 5 foot 7 inches tall and I may exercise nearly every day vigorously, but that by no means equates to me being deemed as healthy. Sounds strange, doesn't it? I do not smoke, I do not do drugs, I do not eat fried foods/fast foods, and I rarely drink and yet I still have cancer. It does cause one to stop and pause. And, yes, those bleepity bleep bleeps that I describe are cancer cells and boy are they evil little things…a lot like cockroaches and when you see them you know they are multiplying way too quickly.

So, what blindsided me? Obviously, the news that I have cancer again in spite of my best efforts to be healthy. Last time took my breath away literally and I needed a paper bag to breath into to stop hyperventilating. I thought hearing the news again might somehow be something that I could more easily handle, but boy was I wrong. Knowing it came back might be even more scary to me than hearing it for the first time.

When I got the news that I got it a third time, it was even harder than the previous two times, because it had spread to many places in my bones. It is then called metastatic stage 4 breast cancer. We will dig into that lovely experience a little later on, but suffice it to say, the news rocked my world.

Let me take you where I was for a moment when I thought I was cancer free:

I just finished rocking the best weekend of my life at my favorite mountain bike race. This race makes 18 years in a row out of the possible 20 years that it has existed. The 24 - Hours in Old Pueblo is an endurance mountain bike race and one of the most highly regarded in the world. The race sells out within minutes of registration opening each year.

This race was one of the few where I had a stellar 4th place podium finish. Over 100 mountain bike miles completed and 6 laps (I'd only ever done 3 laps before!), I got to race with my bad ass hubby, have the world's most well-known and largest 24-hour race dedicated to me, and got to be surrounded by amazing people who for some freaky reason enjoy my company. Can you believe it? A mere mortal, totally not a professional athlete, and a whole entire race is dedicated to me. Surreal. Crazy. Insane. Way cool. Really? It's never been dedicated to a non-professional before? OK, kind of legendary but still very *very* weird.

Ohhhh and there is this guy named Lance Armstrong and his teammates from WEDU (George Hincapie, Christian Vande Velde, Dylan Casey, and JB Hager) who interviewed me on the highly listened to Stages podcast. WEDU is the answer to a question. The question is, "Who believes that the most meaningful revelations emerge at the far edge of your limits -that there are flashes of self-truth in moments of suffering? WEDU. These folks believe WEDU is a mindset rooted in the belief that every challenge ignites a spark of growth and change. In fact, they choose courage over comfort zone, adventure over apathy, and hardcore over ho-hum. This crew of athletes created a movement and a podcast rooted in these philosophies. Do you notice how aligned they are with how I think and act? If you do not see if yet then keep reading. Well shoot, keep reading anyway!

Did I mention that this race we attended is always dedicated to a professional athlete, and it was dedicated to me? No, I am not a professional athlete. I am just an ordinary girl who happens to be highly competitive and likes to push her limits. It was a great race. The best ever.

The dirt was perfect hero dirt (in mountain biking lingo that means it had just rained which made the ground hard packed and fast to ride on) and the temperatures were never cold! Seriously how does it get any better?!

Then a few days later, I fly to Utah to do the coolest interview of my life for a job with a company President and his COO on the ski slopes of Sundance for 5 hours and it dumps stellar powder along with being empty of people! Oh wait, did I mention that we were not eating a meal over the interview or sitting across from one another at a desk but skiing? Ya, it was pretty high up on the awesome meter.

Fast-forward to a day later, my husband and I are celebrating our anniversary. We find a lump on my breast that I thought was impossible to have, because hello, almost nothing on my chest is actually mine anymore from round 1 of cancer! Quickly freaking out, hyperventilating, mind spinning and tears streaming when the radiologist looks at the ultrasound and says yes, looks like cancer and you have a questionable lymph node as well. Both should be biopsied. This is the part where you hold it all together and then walk out to your car to throw up.

A few days later the biopsy is done and holy guacamole...could that be more painful? The Lidacain didn't do shit and they shotgun a needle into your armpit loud and hard multiple times. Thank goodness the one lymph node in question comes back clear but the lump on my breast is definitely cancer.

Unfortunately, warrior or not, I begin to wonder how far it has spread and where is it in my body. Everything you read about and learn about cancer says that if it comes back, it takes over fast. Is my body riddled with it? What can I do to make whatever lies ahead better for the people in my life? They are not fragile but many will not be able to handle going through this rollercoaster with me again. My mind was processing and racing and of course with no answers and no plan, I felt completely out of control.

Everything happens for a reason. Dylan Casey is a retired American professional cyclist who used to ride for the U.S. Postal Service alongside Lance Armstrong in the Tour de France and many other races. Dylan Casey just happened to be in town on the day I learned I had cancer again and he had asked if I could meet up with him for his brief stint in town. Now, I had just met him in the Old Pueblo race, and we were celebrating my being cancer free and figuring out the next chapter in my consulting business just two weeks earlier. I couldn't pull myself together to even speak with him on the phone without sobbing. I was scared and I wasn't sure what to do about it. I decided that just being honest with him would be best, because I am not a very good liar and telling him I needed to wash my hair wasn't likely believable as to why I did not want to see him or anyone for that matter. After sharing the news and letting him convince me to meet up we did have a great cup of coffee. He shared some really great stuff about cutting edge ways to make my body less inhabitable by cancer cells. He introduced to me the Keto diet.

Following my amazing visit with Dylan, I saw a book in my Naturopathic Doctor's (N.D.) office called *Keto and Cancer*. I decided to order it right away and get started. I was grateful for the hope that was now present and that was helping me find positivity in a world of fear.

Not much was in my control, however, if I had hope then I could at least start to keep my mind busy with things that I could control while I waited for answers and a strategy.

I also decided to move forward and get my medical marijuana card. So, for some reason I felt like I was doing something naughty and was embarrassed to even ask about the benefits of CBD or THC on fighting cancer. I guess I have always fallen in the camp of "potheads are just not me" and low and behold, I had stagnated on that learning opportunity up until that point. Once I got past the embarrassment, then my N.D.

walked me through the process of obtaining and qualifying for a card in Arizona. Once it came in, I was nervous to even tell Mike (my husband) about it. I thought he'd be furious and he wouldn't understand that there are actual studies linking decreased inflammation with cancer cell death. I underestimated him, because he completely supported my exploring this and even trying it to calm my intense anxiety on this roller-coaster.

Honestly, I also was in and out of panic attacks wanting to scream, "I am not ready to die yet!!". I started to think about the things I really want to do, the impacts I want to make, the little sweet faces of my toddlers, or even my poor hubby who does not deserve to be going through this again...and last time I believe I relied on a half of a Xanax from time to time, but this time, I wanted to bite the head off a THC laced gummy bear and just let it chill me out. So, I set out to learn. I talked to a few friends and then went to the dispensary with an open mind ready to ask a lot of questions.

When I walked in, I was surprised to learn that you are greeted and then screened by some very kind and professional folks and then they let you back behind the locked door to what I would call "the store". Someone greets you and then takes your order. In my case, the poor fella had to explain the differences between the 6 different methods you can use or take CBD/THC and then had to remind me how THC has both upper effects or downer effects and the different doses. I already know I'm a lightweight and hate being out of control, so we determined that the absolute smallest dose would work just fine. I learned about a topical lotion that can help decrease swelling and pain and I jumped all over that for my sore muscles post riding.

OK, I now had a coping mechanism, although, honestly, after several experiences with trial and error, I learned that at best a micro micro dose of sativa, which is supposed to be energizing, is all it takes to calm me down and make me sleep like a baby. So that means that I nibble on an ear of a gummy bear or a toe – ha ha! I also learned that even a nibble of something called Indica is enough to put me to sleep for days. For me, indica is like drugging an elephant to sleep. Everyone reacts differently and my reaction to most medications is extreme so it figures that THC is no different.

At this point I still have no answers or strategies but at least I'm calm and about to embark on "operation starve those cancer cells so they can't grow". We'll talk about that in a hot minute.

Let's go back to my experience with the hotel company executives that I had been skiing with and contemplating working for or at least consulting on how to improve their top line revenues. I called the company President, whom I had become quite fond of and let him know that it would be best if I helped them to find a suitable leader to guide them moving forward, because I was just re-diagnosed with breast cancer and I didn't know what that journey was going to look like. The only thing I knew with certainty was that it would be very messy and it would not be fair to them to have to maneuver this craziness.

Now most people would process all of that and start backing up slowly (figuratively) and trying to find a way to run. However, Joel Sybrowsky is wired to look a challenge square in the eyes and say, "Let's do this!". He shared with me that I am now family and that we are on this journey together if I'll let him be.

You see, what he had discerned is that even if I worked part time, it would be more impactful than most people working full time (wow, not sure how he figured this out from one day of skiing but he is correct). What I learned over the next year is that by opening my heart up to the Lodging Dynamics family, I would be lifted by their strength, prayers, and passion for respecting human dignity and that we would grow together.

Over the three years that we worked together Joel was generous beyond comprehension. As you will see coming up, there were times of surgery, times of chemo, 7 weeks of radiation, and eventually 7 weeks of hyperbaric chamber time and more surgery and then covid hit. Needless to say, my ability to travel was clearly minimal and for a hotel company that had always been headquarter centric in Provo, UT, it was a lot to ask for the company to suddenly be skillset centric and not care about geography or ability to travel. The needs of the company changed and we both knew that at some point the nomad in me would move on and continue to dedicate my time to writing this book and to helping more epic humans to find happiness. The parting letter that Joel wrote to the 800 employees of Lodging Dynamics Hospitality Group summarizes well, our story:

Letter to All LDHG Employees regarding Victoria's Departure

When I met Victoria four years ago in the Sundance ski resort parking lot, I immediately knew she was special. It was a mid-winter morning but if I hadn't been wearing a ski jacket and trudging through snow, I would have thought someone lit off Fourth of July fireworks. She just has that way about her. Having Victoria join LDHG was a no-brainer and a few hours later she, Scott McAllister and I discussed that opportunity at Bear Claws' Cabin, about 10,000 ft in elevation atop the resort. It was an epic beginning to an energetic and fun business relationship that started off with Victoria leading sales, then shifting to the COO position and more recently as president of the company.

Every now and again Victoria would remind me that she's a professional nomad—she doesn't usually stay in one position or company very long. We are now living that fact. As we've counseled together, given the trajectory of the company and the need for full-time leadership in the president's role, as well as Victoria's many other remarkable pursuits, today is the day for new leadership. Thankfully, she will continue to consult with us—so that association we've enjoyed so much will continue in our business and personal lives.

One of the things I appreciated the most about Victoria was the transition when we planned to have Victoria take over my role as president April 1 last year. When we set that date, we hadn't heard of Covid-19 and didn't know it was going to turn into a global pandemic. As April 1 neared, many of our national institutions shut down and in the wake of all of it, travel and hotels shut down too. And yet we proceeded with a seamless leadership transition in the depth of a severe recession we had never before imagined. In the worst of times her strengths shone through. She showed unflinching leadership. She was positive. She was dauntless. She found things to be happy about (which was, as you know, extraordinary). She caused us all to think we could succeed. More remarkably, Victoria had her own personal health challenges she needed to face, as well as being a wife and mother to twin girls shut out of school. And yet, what she did helped us experience the pandemic in a way no other management company could—with positive anticipation and excitement about our future.

It's with these grateful feelings we go forward having been made better by Victoria Cramer. We thank her sojourning with us in the company. We now look toward a bright future with new leadership. And Victoria will be at our side, cheering and being part of our next achievements.

I am personally grateful for my friendship with this amazing woman. She has blessed my life. I wish her, Mike, Parker and Ryan every success and plan to have a front row seat to their wonderful lives long into the future.

Joel Sybrowsky
Vice Chairman, Lodging Dynamics Hospitality Group

So, with the support of a newfound friendship, fruitful work to keep my mind occupied, my amazing friends and family by my side, I began to tackle all that was in store.

That first week of being blindsided again was honestly not much different than the first time I learned I had cancer, only this time, what was paralyzing was wondering if it was all throughout my body and not knowing if I had a fighting chance at survival. It was time to start getting answers, choosing the right team with the right capabilities to do the best work, and it was time for a strategy. Just remember from my first battle, "Victoria with a strategy is unstoppable". I was remembering those words and hoping that a strategy would become clear quickly.

CHAPTER 2 - TAKING CONTROL

"Control your own destiny or someone else will"
– Jack Welch

The hardest part of any speed bump is the waiting. It is depleting and frustrating and terrifying not to have answers and not to know what, if anything you can do to improve the situation. I would challenge even the most impressive meditators to live in the moment and tell me they have no fear or frustrations during this phase. No doubt it is brutal.

What I did not realize is that this time around would bring more mixed perspectives, doctors not agreeing on the diagnosis much less treatment recommendations. Also, that there would be people who were on my team for the first fight that did not want to be on my team for the second fight. So many emotions to contend with and so much information to sort through to find the best path forward.

The only thing that I could grapple with was that I had cancer again and this time around it had to be my fault. It is not rational but it was how I could try to take control. I just needed to own it and to believe that it was my fault, because then I could do something about it.

Author Dr. Jason Selk, has written several great books. He coaches athletes to better performance and uses his techniques to help not only professional athletes but anyone who wants to live a longer disease-free life. OK, I do not know if he would classify his works this way, but I sure do. He wrote a book called *Relentless Solution Focus* and when I read it, I realized quickly how important it is to move past the shock and move to solutions.

You see, Dr. Selk has researched the fact that everyone comes programmed to think in terms of problems and problem avoidance, but *that* wiring is only serving the cave man. In 2022 we have come much further than your average caveman. Thinking about problems is just going to release cortisol which is your fight or flight adrenaline state. Over prolonged time this actually leads to more health problems like heart disease and cancer. Dr. Selk has worked to help people understand that if you can quickly move from worrying about your problem to truly being solution centric, then you can stop that cortisol state and keep your body functioning in a healthy state.

I can truly attest to the mind's ability to switch paths and to calm itself by focusing on solutions and your body and nerves by focusing on actions within its control. When you train your mind to do this then you quickly shift to a euphoric state or a clear-headed state at a minimum. This is easily said, but not so easily done when the stakes are high and the intensity of the situation dire. It is a trick I learned, unfortunately, from my first battle where I wanted to "turn off" my emotions. I wanted to be in control so the people around me would have less stress. Ultimately, by learning to "flip the switch", I could move from the racing emotional heart to the calm levelheaded solution-focused heart.

What I never realized until I read "Relentless Solution Focus" was that I was in training for battle number 2 and that I had been training my brain over that time. So, how did I take control this time during another phase of insanity? Well, let's talk about food and just how insanely you can change physiology and the way your body functions. I always knew food was important and I never truly appreciated just how impactful every bite could be.

In the absence of knowledge about my cancer and what fight I had ahead, I decided to engross myself in understanding how cancer grows and more importantly how to stop it.

After 2 days of reading and researching what the keto lifestyle is and how it works, I decided it was the way I needed to live at least until I had answers and a strategy. The first thing I had to do was learn that some people stay on a keto diet for years or a lifetime. For me it was not going to be a lifestyle but rather something I do randomly to clean out my system and for now to slow any cancer growth. I learned there is importance in doing regular fasting, which is essentially a similar concept of starving the body of sugars.

Before we dive into keto, I will share with you that with the years of battling that I have experienced, fortunately, new scientific discoveries have also emerged. Once I learned about my stage 4 cancer diagnosis, a year after finishing battling for a second time, it was discovered that certain blood types do better on a keto diet and certain blood types do better on a plant-based diet. I am A+ and do much better on a plant-based diet, which explains why keto was so bloody hard for me.

The crucial component when fighting cancer or any disease really, is to decrease inflammation and to improve liver function. Sugar is the primary source of so many issues. Sugar leads to leaky gut, bloating, and inflammation. Doesn't that sound awful? Leaky gut just means you have imbalances in your stomach which overtime could lead to inflammation propagating up to the digestive track or down to the intestines. It's complicated and has many manifestations but ultimately keeping your gut healthy and happy is a good thing.

If you decide to embark on a lifestyle change, the one commonality you'll find is the need to cut out sugar. There are also many ways to improve gut and liver health and function and fortunately lemon water and green tea are a great start and I love them both. I digressed, but it's important to know that in battle number 2, I did not have this information. I did what I could to control my outcome. Keto made a big impact.

OK, let's get to it.

Let's start with some basics about what keto is and our body's ability to go into ketosis. Ketosis is a metabolic state which causes your body to burn fat instead of carbs for energy. Ironically, it means that you have to have a very low carb and high fat diet. The part that scares most people is that it goes against everything we've been taught about eating things daily like meats and eggs. With this concept it's about taking sugars and carbs out, and putting fats in.

So, the amazing thing that I've learned and experienced through my blood work and later through my sister's 2-year keto lifestyle (and blood work) is that this process actually lowered our cholesterol. I was worried about the effect on my heart but in my case what does it matter if my heart is strong if I'm dead from cancer.

The interesting thing is that cutting out sugar and carbs actually appears to strip out and clean arteries. So, with a new day and new information, I was ready to give it a try. It meant that I had to read every label and before I describe what happened to me, I should share with you that there is sugar in darn near everything! The surprising thing was most seasonings for tacos, fajitas, gravies, all have sugar in them. There is not a single brand or type of bratwurst in the U.S. without sugar in it. The biggest changes for me were in cutting out fruit (yes, at first all fruit), breads, alcohol, and lattes with milk (ugh this was brutal…I was having a tall/ small mocha every day…just one but still).

I read about the power of completely changing what you have in your home and getting your family to do it with you, so my husband agreed but no way were we going to get our little 5-year-olds on board. That was fine.

So, getting into ketosis or registering your ketones in the optimum range was hard and at first, I used some pee sticks to check, but eventually realized that getting a ketone tester was crucial. It is a little device much like a diabetic would use to prick their finger and then get drops of blood on a stick. Then the machine tells you if you're in ketosis. The first three days for me were rough and they call it the keto flu, because you feel sick like you would if you had the flu. Some people get into ketosis faster than others. I have heard that by including fasting you can expedite that process. I simply worked hard trying to cut out sugar. Let me just say it sucked.

I had a good attitude about it, but it made me so weak and super tired and it is because the body is essentially trying to break an addiction. Those who have had to wean themselves off caffeine or alcohol probably know exactly what I'm saying. My body went through sweats, nausea, headaches and weak muscles. I had no strength on a bike and I was feeling like an elephant was sitting on me. OK, I know that makes me sound emo (just a modern way of saying dramatic), but I'm telling you it was brutal. Once I broke through into ketosis and my body started using fats for energy, I felt like a cloud had lifted.

So, at first, I was craving bananas and that was torture. I swear my brain wanted banana cream pie, peanut butter banana sandwiches, banana smoothies, and anything else banana you can think of. The weird thing is that I never really ate bananas at all, so I wasn't sure if it was mental. As a side note, I finally found a sugar free banana pudding recipe and that worked to fix that weird craving. I also later learned that often your body craves something that it needs. In this case, I didn't realize it but I was low in potassium and some crazy craving was trying to fix that. Is that wild?! Yes. The body is amazing but we do not often have the skills and awareness to recognize the language being spoken or shared.

Keto for me only lasted for 3-months and I won't forget how much of an impact it had. It was a "Hail Mary" for me. I was not sure if it was needed but it was at least something to occupy my brain while we tried to sort through what was ahead.

Within 1 week, I dropped an insane 10 pounds! The following week I dropped 5 more pounds! And in the end after surgery, we learned that in that short time, the size of the cancer had shrunk!

Let me say that again. The doctors had measured the tumor size prior to surgery and what they removed was measurably smaller. Some would say it was God and some would say it was the universe. I am confident that science was right that cancer can be changed and slowed by removing sugar. My story is not the first like this and I am grateful for Dylan Casey putting this science in my hands. I am also grateful for the support network that gave me great recipes to help keep me focused.

Within a short period of time, I found I was not hungry. This is probably part of the reason I was losing weight so fast. So, in my case, I had to eat more fats and overall, just more food. Nut butters became a staple snack for me because I could toss a pouch of unsweetened almond butter into my cycling jersey pocket or my purse and snack when I knew I was burning calories. I finally stabilized my weight and kept it at the 15 pounds down.

This is how amazing it can be to try something hard and terrifying and at the same time share it with vulnerability to the world...ok or maybe just to your "network" no matter what size that it is for you. I shared my 2nd battle and that I was trying keto and holy guacamole, I learned of so many people quietly doing this with success!

Mind you, I had never heard of it before; as many others had not heard of it either, they asked a lot of questions. The reality is that it is so drastic that nearly no one on my "team" decided to take on the keto challenge with me. I was fine with that because it is no one else's battle to fight.

I'm sure you're thinking, "and you had your husband doing it with you!"? Ha Ha Ha. OK, keep laughing because this is a funny one. So, that sweet man lasted 1 week. I do not know if he ever went into ketosis fully or if his poor mind just had to torture him, but he was miserable. He wanted to do it with me but his being miserable is an understatement. He was craving everything! The keto food rules were so complicated that it scared him and he just wanted to get back to eating carbs. I could tell he was tortured while I was excited to be learning and trying new things. So, we talked about how it was not important for him to walk in my shoes and that him being miserable does me no good at all. I swear he did the happy dance. For a man who shows very little emotion, it was like he was set free! He sneaked out of the house the next day and ate like 6 donuts and 2 bagels before lunch! I think he washed it down with a venti mocha from Starbucks. He came home smiling from ear to ear and was trying to hide it. I'm laughing hard just picturing his face. When I asked if he was doing ok, he could not hold it in anymore and he fessed up to going nuts with carbs and sugars. I nearly fell out of my chair laughing so hard. He felt like absolute crap the next day - the sugar hangover was real but he was free and that freedom made him happy. Fortunately, I had him try it so he could understand the physiology behind it and that is all it took for him to sample several yummy treats I had started making that were 100% keto. We were aligned and learning together which is what mattered most.

So anytime you put yourself out there, whether talking with friends or over social media, you impact or imprint on someone else's life. Your actions matter. Your outlook matters. Your words matter. When you are facing your kick in the gut, it is fairly safe to say that it is easy to lose sight of the importance of your reaction because survival mode and self-protection mode kicks in. However, you do have unintended impact and you should remember that.

This was not my first rodeo and although terrified, I was blocking out fear with curiosity and control. I had shared openly that I had cancer again, only that I did not even have a plan yet because there were too many unanswered questions.

In the meantime, I was trying on this keto lifestyle to see if by chance it could save my life. Well, holy wow, was I surprised at how many people decided that trying it with me would be a good idea. Several people bowed out quickly because it is not for the weak - that is for sure. My mom and my youngest sister who have struggled with weight most of their adult lives decided to try it. I was so proud of my mom for making it through a month. Ultimately, even though I shared some pretty darn good keto English muffin recipes; they just aren't an English muffin and that craving wasn't going to be held back. Ha!

However, my sister, had tried many "diets" plus she had very hungry teenage boys at home, as well as a fast-paced work life, so honestly, she was not the one that I would say could win the "keto challenge" and she killed it! Check this out, at the time of this book, she has been living the keto lifestyle for 3 years and has lost over 50 pounds! She has since coached others to be successful with the lifestyle and created quite the following of keto loving folks.

So, now think about that ripple effect. I shared in a spirit of curiosity and intrigue versus a place of sadness or doom, and it impacted some people short term and others long term, and then they impacted others and so on.

If you are thinking keto could be your solution then how about I share a couple of tricks that helped me a ton?

1. After you're in ketosis, you will be able to enjoy a few berries each day and each one will be quite satisfying! Strawberries, raspberries, blueberries, or even some dried cranberries or raisins won't kick you out of ketosis.

2. Iced coffee with some almond milk or coconut milk is a great solution for you coffee drinkers.

3. I began using Pinterest to save recipes that I loved. If you have a sweet tooth then try making a keto chocolate cake or keto friendly no bake chocolate cookies with nuts or peanut butter. They are also called fat bombs because of the good fats in the peanut butter, and who doesn't love dark chocolate?

4. Sugar replacements can be challenging and everyone has their favorites. To me they all had a bad after taste until I discovered Swerve and monk fruit. I love both the granular, the brown sugar, and the confectioner for baking and everyday use. The simplicity is that you use the same measurement of Swerve or monk fruit as you would for traditional sugar, so it made baking recipes easy.

5. After you're in ketosis, you can have an alcoholic beverage a day and be fine. However, you have to figure out which alcohols spike your sugar. Prosecco

instead of champagne, tequila, vodka, or whiskey are just great but only with olives or with club soda or a non-sugar based organic mixture. Fortunately, I love both Prosecco and martinis.

We will tackle this in more detail coming up but let me say right now being a warrior is hugely grounded in mindset. It doesn't mean perfect, but it does mean starting from a place of curiosity and finding something positive to cling to.

OK, I digress, let's go back to my statement about how this cancer growing this time has to have been my own fault. I said it was nots rational but taking responsibility for it helped me to move past the question of "why", which so many people do start off asking and moving to a "So what? What's next?". The faster I could move past the "why" the more prepared I would be to tackle the taking control part. So, I began asking myself to truly reflect on just how "healthy" am I?

I was the gal who although not obese, lived on sugar. I was the gal going through Starbucks drive through up to 2x/day for a sugary drink, the gal who ate and drank a lot of heavily glucose focused foods while riding and racing my bike every day for many hours a day. When not on the bike, I was enjoying cake, cookies, or a brownie often and eating just a bagel or a banana to bolt out the door each day. I was in denial that I was an unhealthy eater, because I didn't eat fast food or fried food and because I would eat a salad once to twice a day. So, I decided to own it and believe that by making changes, I could make an impact.

Before I knew it, I was reminding myself that my life has purpose, my story is important, my dreams count, my voice matters, and I was born to make an impact. I was regaining my footing even though my insides were scared.

CHAPTER 3 - COMPLEXIFICATION

"A positive attitude gives you power over your circumstances instead of your circumstances having power over you." – Joyce Meyer

What is complexification? Well, it is a made-up word that a friend of mine shared and he describes it as the ability to take the simplest concepts and complicate them to the nth degree. This is what cancer journey number two ended up being. I will try to spare you the complex details and yet paint you the picture that is often life as a human; decisions rife with complexification. If nothing else you can get a laugh out of trying to spell it and say it.

Cancer battle number one was the hardest thing I had ever done in my life. Cancer battle number two raised the bar and ended up being the hardest battle I had ever done. I'd be ok if we could level off the hard battles now, but I can tell you that I have loved the journey. Yes, you read that right. If you want to be a warrior then you must learn to love the journey. I have been known to say, after battling cancer twice, "If given the chance, I am now wired with the skills to do it again and again and again." And guess what. I got to do it again. I am doing it again.

I'm going to say two things to you that matter so much when you're in the midst of your own battle:

Love the journey!

And...

Find a way to infuse a little vacation in every day!

Yes, these are Victoria quotes.

You see every day in a warrior's life has to be inspiring. It has to have reward to go with the hard work and the pain. There is no sense in saving it up for milestones, because warriors don't live assuming they'll make those milestones. They live for today; this day. So, infuse a little spark or a little guilty pleasure into each day. Now with that, let's get on with the complexification!

The most resilient people are able to be vulnerable. Vulnerability seems inherent to learning and a learner mindset. I openly shared my fears and I started to explore answers and solutions and to my shock I learned that total strangers were including me in prayer chains. People were fasting and praying. Although I didn't feel worthy of all of this, I did feel like my family was worthy, so I gladly and gratefully accepted prayers from many religions. If you know me, then you know that praying isn't really my thing. However, if you know me, you'll know that instead, I made it my mission to make it the most comfortable experience for everyone around me. It was hard when some turned their backs on me, but honestly, that is a protective mechanism and, in some cases, when people don't know what to say then they just step away. It isn't that they aren't supportive, it's that they are uncomfortable. When I realized this, then it was no longer hard. Instead of worrying about that, I worried about inspiring myself and others every day while I waited to create a plan.

Scientifically, do you know that there is evidence that happiness is tied to having connectedness and by feeling your impact on the world, on your friendships, or in your job? The happiest of people feel a sense of purpose. So, why then, would I not focus on the things *in* my control? So, I was determined to inspire other people by getting them outdoors.

You see, I've always felt that when you get outside you get inspired. I decided to throw down a get outdoors challenge for 30-days. I called it the May Movement Challenge. I created a Facebook Group called Get Outside Get Inspired and I asked my network of about 1,000 people who would join me? Do you know there were about three hundred people that committed to the journey and the challenge! I asked that they post pictures of themselves living life loudly outdoors throughout the 30 days. Lots of people posted pictures of themselves walking, running, biking, gardening, skiing, and playing with their kids.

The challenge made such an impact that shockingly three years later as I was being introduced to speak to a Rotary Club, my friend told the story about the challenge and the kind of person I am to focus on other people during my fight. He told them how it changed *his* life and he hasn't stopped exercising since.

During this same timeframe, there was a gentleman who worked for me as a General Manager of a hotel in Colorado. He was going through a rough patch in life and floundering. It wasn't a speed bump but he was feeling a bit of despair. He took up the challenge and do you know because he kept it going, he became a runner and started inspiring others to run. He didn't know that he was building a base and foundation for resilience. When Covid 19 hit, he became one of the most resilient leaders in the hotel industry because he had the keys to lifting his spirits and his overall happiness.

I challenged him to write about his experiences and to share it with others and he did. Andrew Debruzzi, you are resilient! Here is what he wrote:

This thirty-day challenge changed my life for the better. I felt like I was starting to become depressed and was under a significant amount of stress for a number of reasons. The pandemic hit my industry and my wife's career particularly hard, my family suffered the loss of a close friend, and the everyday expectations felt never ending. I had tried to exercise regularly a few weeks prior to get out of my funk but I just couldn't get myself out of bed.

One day Victoria reached out to me and during our conversation she suggested to me that I should consider exercising every day for 30 days to shake things up. I hadn't completed 5 days straight of exercise in my recent memory, let alone 30 days. My mindset was to just take one day at a time, reach 7 days and then after 7 days, keep going for 7 more and so on. I started running every day, short runs that were approximately 1-2.5 miles. This was a struggle the first week or so and then I started enjoying the time to myself, clearing my mind. I was feeling less and less depressed, started gaining energy, and was not so physically drained at the end of the day. I found this to be sort of a paradox in a sense because I was getting up 30 minutes earlier and so, in my mind, I was losing sleep but feeling more energized. By about the 2nd or 3rd week of this routine I felt more productive at work and more present at home with my family. I think I ended up making it about 32 or 33 days straight of daily exercise.

After making this exercise part of a daily routine I noticed that when I occasionally had to miss a day or two of running my mood was negatively impacted. At this point, I realized that I needed exercise in my life for not only my physical health but my mental health as well. The following few months I kept running daily and even took my runs on vacation which was fun to see new places and running routes. Several months later I started doing longer runs approximately 5-7 miles at a time. The longer runs were a result of a couple of friends who had seen my progress and pushed me to do more. I am pleased to say this challenge changed my life and I will be running my 1st half marathon this summer. I am forever grateful for my friend, and mentor, for pushing me and inspiring me to do this life changing 30-day challenge.

OK, so, at this point we have me focusing on others but where are we at with the complexification? Let's dig into that.

So medically, up to this point, all we had was confirmation that I had cancer again. Just like with my first battle with cancer, the only person other than my husband that was worrying probably even more was my naturopathic doctor, Dr. Daniel Rubin. He kept asking questions that I knew I needed answers to, but I didn't know how to get them. You see, the oncologist from my first battle literally abandoned me. I will never know why and my gut tells me it was fear. When I wasn't getting returned calls from her or her office, I decided to reach out to a friend to see if Mayo Clinic would be willing to take on my case and in a hurry. Now I mention the in a hurry part, because if you've ever tried to work with Mayo Clinic, then you'll know that the word hurry isn't part of their vocabulary. They are a big institution and they are incredible at much of what they do, but getting your foot in the door as a new patient is very hard. Fortunately, my friend is an oncologist and he was able to get me an appointment with their best breast cancer oncologist. Unfortunately, it was still a bit of time until that would happen.

We were able to get a petscan scheduled to determine where the cancer was in my body. The results were expedited and for once a radiologist talked to me within 15 minutes of having the scan. She held my hand and she told me it was only in my breast or rather in the tissue sitting over my fake breast. She didn't see it anywhere else in my body. I cried. She cried. I went for a mountain bike ride and screamed loudly in the desert to pretty much no one in particular "Thank You!" and I think I yelled, "I've got this! Bring on the battle!".

Mayo Clinic started responding and I was on the phone answering what seemed like 15,000 questions about every detail of my life and every surgery I'd ever had and questions about which hospitals I had been at and could they get records. Now this all sounds normal, but you guys, with all of the surgeries I'd had and the oodles of anesthesia and chemo, I couldn't answer all of the questions. In fact, one hospital had changed names so I started to question my sanity when I couldn't find that hospital on google to save my life. Funny right? Not so much. Seriously it was frustrating. She said they would work hard to collect all my records as quickly as they could so that I could have a visit with the doctor.

In the meantime, we decided to start seeking a different surgeon from the one we had previously, because we learned that the reason it was possible for me to get breast cancer again was because some breast tissue was left behind by the first surgeon. It is nearly impossible to get everything but the concern that my husband and I had was if it was left behind before then maybe we should be looking at using a different set of eyes for this next surgery. The surgeon we met with was very matter of fact and said that I would need to find a radiologist, because whether chemo was needed or not, radiation would likely need to happen after surgery.

We had some decisions to make about surgery:

1. Either we do a major surgery and take the implants out and have the surgeon really go over me with a fine-tooth comb and try to be sure no breast tissue is left behind… or

2. We have him operate soon and get the mass out and then plan to tackle a potential for chemo or radiation. He wasn't even sure whether or not to call it a new cancer or a reoccurrence. He probably wouldn't know because he wouldn't have the DNA details from the

first mass that was removed in my double mastectomy nearly 4 years earlier.

What would you do? I felt completely lost in these decisions because we were told this situation is really rare. Usually if cancer comes back, it comes back everywhere and fast and usually not in some small swath of breast tissue that was missed.

We decided to move forward with surgery quickly (within 3 weeks of seeing the surgeon) to get it out. While making this decision, Mayo Clinic finally told me that their oncologist would see me for a consultation. His earliest appointment was for after surgery would be complete, which was about a month from that point. I'm thinking, "ya, don't rush, cancer can wait for you doctors." YES, I'm being sarcastic ha ha.

The surgeon recommended that I meet with a radiologist as soon as possible, because I would most certainly need radiation. He made an incredible recommendation, and saying this is one of the best doctors he's ever met. Well, ok, then, I like hearing this bit of news! This doctor actually got me in to see him within 48 hours! Wow, can I tell you, this was a delight and shocking too because there has been nothing fast about fighting cancer or getting appointments.

So, you may know this if you read my first book and if not, let me get you up to speed on how I work. I have an equation that has always made me successful at strategy execution.

A Powerful Team + A Solid Strategy + Flawless Execution = Rock Star Success

Well, at this point in the first fight, I was much farther along than at this stage in my second fight - so I was starting to feel frustrated. I had my fair share of challenges in the first battle in choosing doctors for my super powerful team. As a reminder, I met with a couple dozen doctors to finally land on the right team who seemed willing to work together and who all seemed to listen and hear what my objectives were. I know it sounds crazy but most that I met with didn't seem to care that I had goals. They all had a certain approach and weren't willing to explore alternatives with me until I found the needle in the haystack. But once the team was chosen the strategy fell into place.

Exploring The Right Team

Much like my first battle, this time around, I was feeling frustrated with how difficult it was to form the right team. This particular radiologist that I met with made an enormous difference. Although in the end he did not "make it" on my team, I am still profoundly grateful for his tenacity.

Armed with what imaging I had and the pathology (like the DNA or gene make-up of this cancer) my husband and I went to meet with the radiologist. I had done a heck of a lot of google searching to understand radiation and the two types that exist. I knew enough to be a giant pain in the ass. Have you ever done so much research on your own on a topic totally not your forte' but you're convinced you could get a PhD on the topic now? Yup, that was me.

So, what I had discovered was that I had two radiation treatment options:

1. Proton Therapy – where the radiation is targeted and focuses only on what is mapped to be radiated.

2. Photon Therapy – where the beams of radiation go straight through you and likely will hit other organs and tissue that don't need to be radiated.

This radiologist I met with was as warm as a rock. He was very matter of fact and this scared the shit out of me. You see up to this point, I had heard that I would definitely need to do radiation this time around. However, after surgery and maybe a few weeks of radiation, I should be able to just jump back into my life as I knew it. OK, or maybe that's what I wanted to believe.

He told us that my situation appeared unique. He said that this cancer could be called a stand-alone cancer or it could be called a re-occurrence. I thought it was semantics and didn't understand why it mattered or why he appeared so frightened for me. He told me that I should hit this hard and go through another double mastectomy essentially and have them really clean out my chest wall to be sure that there is no more breast tissue left behind. He told me that he would bet that the oncologist at Mayo would tell me to do chemo. He would recommend that too. Then he'd recommend six weeks of radiation where we hit lymph nodes and entire chest wall.

Honestly, I found myself staring at him like he was a crazy person. The thought of going through all of that sounded extreme. There was absolutely no way was I doing chemo again. He was now talking to me about things that I wasn't prepared to wrap my head around.

I changed the subject and decided to focus on his specialty of radiation. I asked if he had access to Proton Therapy because I definitely wanted that option. He said no. He didn't and he told me that I didn't want that because it's too new and not researched enough to gamble my life with it. He proceeded to tell me that I'm on my reserve parachute and that most people don't get to fight a second time. He added he would give me no more than 3 years to live because of how fast the cancer returned after having done as much chemo as I had done previously. I was angry.

I was so angry. How dare he put a timeline on my life! How dare he presume to know the outcome!

He asked if I even had a radiology appointment at Mayo. He asked if I realized that I wouldn't likely be approved by my insurance for Proton treatment? He stated that they really only give priority for the machine to children or young adults. He said it's in very high demand and there are more people than available treatment spots for the few machines in the state.

I thanked him for his time. I told him that I would contact him if I decided to move forward with him. There was no way that was happening.

On the drive home, my husband, Mike, told me how much he liked this guy and that he was impressed with his knowledge and that he didn't sugar coat any of it. I'm pretty sure I was shooting daggers out of my eyeballs and I simply said, "I'm not using him or anyone else who tries to tell me how long I have to live". I think Mike said I was overreacting ha ha.

So, that appointment was in the morning. At around 1pm I see that the radiologist is calling me. I let it go to voicemail. On his voicemail he asked me to please call him because he wanted to know what hospital my first surgery was at. I was annoyed and ignored him.

He tried calling me again and this time he said it's urgent. I saw nothing worth responding to, so I ignored him again.

Next, I received a text from him and he asked me to call him on his personal cell at any hour and that he isn't trying to scare me but rather that he has gone over every detail of my chart. He really was missing 2 important puzzle pieces:

1. The pathology from the first surgery (not the biopsy but the actual surgery)

2. The report stated that I had a BRCA gene testing done but he doesn't see the results

In my head, I'm thinking what the heck? Who is this guy? Why is he suddenly obsessed with me? Is it because he thinks I'm playing hard to get? I'm not, I'm seriously just not going to work with you because I have to click with the people I work with. They can have a scientific brain and no bedside manner but there needs to be a modicum of mutual respect.

That being said, I was kind of moved by his OCD tendency. I decided to text him back and he pleaded with me to call him. I figured I had nothing to lose and only insights to gain, unless of course he blurted out more of what I didn't want to hear. I called.

This amazing human apologized and asked if we could start over. He told me that he had hunted down my genetic testing and that if no one had told me yet, that I have a gene mutation called a CK2 (pronounced Check Two) and that this mutation makes it hard for my cells to repair themselves. It makes me highly susceptible to both breast cancer and colon cancer. He said he believes this to be a new cancer, which makes it better than a reoccurrence. He said it gives me more of a fighting chance. Based on this, he wanted me to know he agreed with my decision to pursue Mayo Clinic radiation and oncology. If I was not eligible for Proton Radiation, he would love to be my radiologist and would promise to be the best doctor possible for me. He said one last thing that he knew I would not want to hear but he told me I really did need to be prepared to do both radiation and chemo again. The phone call was insightful and terrifying.

Remember the part where I said "I am not doing chemo ever again!". Well, I moved to saying, "Please, please, please if there is a kind higher power, don't make chemo have to happen again". I believe I gagged at the notion, because just the thought of it is enough to cause a warrior to throw up from the trigger memories. Well, that phone call turned out to be worth taking.

Racing Bikes to Prep for Surgery

Now that you are getting to know me, you will realize that while I am going through major decisions and research to create a plan, I am also going to keep doing epic stuff. So, you'll recall I had already started a new food strategy with

Keto and I decided it was time to try my hand at a road biking race that was coming up and would land about two days before surgery. Not probably the wisest idea because it would leave my body a bit dehydrated and healing from the race while trying to heal from surgery ha ha. Yup, that's how I roll. I'm not always the sharpest crayon in the box, but I am a determined soul.

My cousins have always been by my side and been some of my biggest cheerleaders, so they said they would do the race with me. Like with any race, you never really know what "with" will equate to or how each person or their bike will respond to the challenge. My friends had warned me ahead of time that this race is notorious for big crashes right out of the gate or right off the start line and in the first 10 miles because so many racers are jockeying for front spots. They warned me to just watch my front wheel, which means, don't run into anyone who slams on their breaks, because then you go down and not the person in front of you.

My cousins and I had decided to just take it easy off the start line since we were smashed in like sardines literally elbow to elbow. It was sketchy to get clipped into my pedals but low and behold once I did, I was able to start a soft pedal (this just means you start pedaling slowly and smoothly). I couldn't look back but was hoping both of them were behind me and once everyone started to spread out, I'd look back to try to spot them.

As we started to climb a long hill, I found myself going way too slowly with the group I was tacked onto, so I decided to pull out and pass them. I looked back and there was my cousin, Randy, but no sign of his wife, Connie. He passed with me and stayed on my wheel. When we got up to the next group, the same thing happened. So, once again, we pull around and passed and headed to the next group ahead. This continued until we were in a good pace line going at a great pace and before you know it, we are half way finished with the race! Now it started to get dicey. My cousin said "c'mon, let's pass this group". He pulled out around me and started pulling us up to the front and then we were off the front going faster than I thought we should be but figure he had a plan. Nope. No plan. It was just the two of us by ourselves working hard for about 10 miles. Ha! Then without a word he pulled off at a rest stop to go to the bathroom.

OK, I was thinking, "Wait a minute, I'm kinda racing here and restroom stops are what the casual rider does, so nope, I'm not stopping. If I have to pee on myself, I will but I'm hoping to be done before that is necessary.". So, now the problem was that I was by myself. In road bike racing, working as a team with a group is always desirable, because the group breaks the wind for each other and you can draft along at a faster pace for longer than you can by yourself.

Are you seeing the problem? I still had a good distance to cover by myself. I kept my pace up and was hoping a good-sized group of riders would come by. I could jump in with them and become a part of their group. Picture a mama duck with a whole line of ducklings behind her. Usually, they don't notice when one more duckling jumps into the line and gets towed along.

Welp. No such luck and now I was getting tired and the heat was kicking in. I think I must have looked a little pathetic going up a long climb because two guys came by me and slowed their speed down so I could jump on and they did a lot of work and coaxing to get me to the top of the climb. It was only about a 4-mile climb but it felt like 10 miles! Once we accomplished that, I knew I could make it the final 10 miles of the race because it was all downhill or flat.

I'll tell you what though, there is something to be said about small wins along the way, teamwork, and an amazing cheer from time to time to pick up your adrenaline and push you farther than you think you can handle. Right when I was starting to fade again, I looked up to see my amazing husband, Mike, and our little ladies, Parker & Ryan, cheering *Go Mama Go!* Parker is incredibly honest and she said, "The other racers are all in front of you, mom, but you can get them!" ha ha ha ha.

So, I raced 62 miles. It was incredible. Normally to race 62 miles, I'd need a lot of hydration and a lot of calories. On Keto, your body is used to using your fat stores for energy instead of needing glucose. For that entire race, all I needed were electrolytes in my water, some pickle juice, and an almond butter pouch. So, I might have craved a cold diet soda afterwards but that was because I was really craving the carbonation, which honestly happens after every endurance race.

This race was my first road race. While I had done a huge amount of mountain bike racing and triathlons, I had yet to race on the road. It reminded me that I can do hard things. It was great for my mind and my soul. Honestly, I can't remember my time, but I remember thinking that it was actually quite solid. I remember I finished in the top 1/3 of all women, which gave me a benchmark.

So, I went into surgery feeling mentally strong and physically strong. The reason that I put that race on the docket was to remind myself exactly what I'm made of and to go into recovering feeling like a winner. Sure, I could have just gone for a walk and watched a good movie, but my winning combination is racing, pushing through pain, and winning.

Winning isn't about being first or being the fastest but it is about doing better than you think you're capable of. In this case, I really hadn't done a road race before and had no idea how I could race that distance and on a special diet. I had to get personal records all along the course to declare myself a winner and that I did.

Complexification Continues

Complexification is what most organizations do. They take something simple, overthink it, stop up or clog the system so there is very little execution that can happen, because they've over complicated every aspect of a process and all in the spirit of trying to put safety measures in place or to create better checks and balances.

Well, complexification of the most insane amounts can often lead to revolutionary thinking and it can also lead to absolute heresy. I'm learning modern medicine absolutely falls into this category of complexification. There is a reason that it's called practicing medicine; it's not called perfected medicine that's for sure and there are major system failures at every turn. This is why it's so important to have an advocate, a sounding board, and a "team" to help you handle the disappointments, failures, and decisions in your decision-making processes. The burden shouldn't rest on your shoulders alone when it comes to medicine and health. Let's face it, your frame or lens is unique and likely not rational if you've been punched in the gut. Stay true to your values and weigh the hefty decisions with your team. They will carry you because they want to!

I have got to describe to you two of the characters on my team, because they are so unique. They are brilliant. They are far from perfect but their ability to read me and "get me" grew over time. These are critical professionals and they've both been at it a long time. For the protection of their identities, I'm going to call them by different names. Mayo Clinic did finally get me in and when they did, I was assigned an oncologist, radiologist, gene therapist, lymphedema specialists, cardiologist, and nutritionist. I may have missed one of the "ists" but you get the idea.

The oncologist, Dr. Onken, is a zany character who doesn't look you in your eyes, has long hair and looks like someone who is planning to do a social experiment on you. He is super analytical, a man of few words, and clearly looks like someone you'd find working on their PhD in a university. He looked at me and said, "I see no reason for chemotherapy in your case. You did all of the hard chemo last time and this looks like something that has already been solved by your having removed the cancer and by doing radiation. Do you have any questions for me?".

OK, seriously? Yes, Yes, Yes…I like this guy! I said, "So the fact that my first cancer was Her2 positive doesn't concern you? Was this one not Her2 positive?". His answer was, "we see no evidence of it in your pathology report". Just to keep you, the reader up to speed, Her2 positive just means that the cancer cells are extra evil and hard to kill because they can communicate and replicate at a very fast rate.

Um. OK. Nice to meet you and goodbye!

At this point, I was seriously doing the happy dance as I walked out of his office thinking I needed to celebrate. Zippity do da, zippity ay, my oh my what a wonderful day! Yup, I sang it loud and proud.

Now, let's move on to the radiologist. Ms. Radford. She came in with fast energy, a lot of positivity and continued to look at her pager. Yes, I just said pager. Now, I was looking at her using that thing and was very concerned. I started wondering if she's so old school that she doesn't know what she's doing and not sure if she's staying up to date on the most current techniques. She seemed "normalish". She loves to hike and does intense amounts of it. Enjoys traveling to far off locations and likes a challenge. And, yet, used a pager. Weird, but I figured maybe I can get past this little oddity? She seemed surprised that Dr. Onken had said no need for chemo. She said, she would need to talk with him about it before beginning radiation because we would really need to do chemo first.

I said, "Well, since I am not doing chemo can we get started with insurance approval of the proton beam radiation, because I would very much like to use that method?". She agreed and said the next step would be to map the area to be radiated, and she explained that the process is quite extensive. The machine is quite precise. I would have a clam-type plastic molded to me; they would tattoo dots on my body where the beams would need to enter each day for about seven weeks.

Yup, they tattooed dots on me in many places both with this radiation and when I battled a third time. I'm almost a Dalmatian now ☺

OK, wait, what?! 7 weeks! 35 treatments?! Is this really necessary? I was told that in my case, we needed no cell to remain behind or it would kill me. We had to get as much as we could on my right side and in the lymph nodes under my arm. The great news was that my heart and lungs shouldn't need to be radiated. It was a lot to digest but it sounded like she knew what she was doing.

Do you know that screechy sound that happens when you slam on the brakes of a car?! Ya, picture that when I get a call a couple of days later from Dr. Onken.

He said to me, "Remember how I said you wouldn't need chemo? Well, we had a bit of a difference of opinion on the topic between radiology, pathology, and oncology. Your case was sent to a review board where it was reviewed for a half day and the board ruled that because of your unique situation, it would be best to do chemo. We will be trying chemo therapies you haven't done and it will be two different kinds for a total of eight rounds."

Pretty sure you could have heard a pin drop, my stomach dropped, and I had to steady myself. I'm glad he told me over the phone. I had so many emotions running through me. Is nausea considered an emotion? Well, it should be.

He went on to explain that I should start chemo in three days. He asked if I wanted to do surgery to get a chemo port and explained that the first type would be very hard on my veins. I said no thank you. It's just eight times. I did not want surgery for a port and then again to remove it later for just eight rounds. He said it would be every three weeks. I also needed a blood draw every time, but if the veins in my left arm did not cooperate, we could use my right arm. That was crazy to hear because I had been told you never use an arm that has the high potential for lymphedema. He laughed and said "That is old school and no real evidence exists either way, but it is hard to get the nurses to do it, so let's hope we don't need to use your right arm."

He said as I approached the end of chemo then I'd go back and meet with radiology. He did need me to get in for a heart exam ASAP to be sure my heart could handle the chemo. I think I just murmured zombie-like yes statements at this point because I was in shock.

I managed to ask a few more questions and learned that there was a low likelihood that I would go from having a cancer that was Her2 positive to having one that was Her2 negative, and the results from pathology were inconclusive. Because of this, it meant we had to treat this as if it were an aggressive cancer. That dumb Her2 word had become something I despise!

Here was the hardest part of the conversation. The doctor explained there is no specific strategy that has been tried and documented to work in a situation like this. Let me just tell you, this wasn't what I was prepared to hear. In my brain, I'm thinking, "Wait, there's no statistic for this. This is a giant guessing game. Seriously? Holy shit balls, I liked the first diagnosis and first battle better for sure, because with that it was this-is-this, that-is-that, and botabing-botabang, you have a strategy that has typically worked."

WELL CRAP

If you know me at all, then you'll know that:

1. I have to have a plan to execute.

2. I'm going to quickly move from problem to solution and from my scared place to my epic warrior place.

Problem: This is all experimental. There are no statistics for this and you won't be able to declare a victory on some prescribed date. Alright, so what?

Solution: You have never minded being the first in positions, in making career moves, or in anything else in life, so why start worrying about being first now? Do you have a rock-solid team to give you the best educated guesses and direction? YES. Are they quirky; just the way you like them? YES.

From this, the plan fell into place; much later than was comfortable, but the plan was:

1. Chemotherapy (8 rounds)

2. Radiation (7 weeks)

3. Likely re-construction needed or at a minimum replacement of radiated implants

I began to chant in my head and sometimes out loud on mountain bike rides, "This will be okay" and as I did, it changed my core.

This Will Be OK! This Will Be OK! This Will Be OK!

We scheduled D-Day for just after my birthday. When they asked to start chemo on June 18th, my birthday, I said,

"Absolutely not. I have some epic stuff to do!" We started chemo on June 20th, 2018.

It was "go" time and the start to the rest of a long and happy life. Let's do this!

CHAPTER 4 – TIME TO SHOW UP

Chemo Round 1: Gemcitabime & Pertruzamab

"Happiness is not a goal; it is a byproduct"
– Eleanor Roosevelt

Eleanor Roosevelt had this right. I exercise every day, not because I have to but because I *get* to. I rise up as fast as I can every morning to catch the sunrise. In the summer, it means that I often have to be up at 4:30am just to be ready to be on my bike before the sun comes up and I pedal fast towards areas where I know I'm likely to see a coyote standing on a hill watching the same sunrise. It's a gift.

Sometimes I walk with a cup of coffee in my hand and I do it because I *can* walk and because if I'm lucky and am up early enough, I catch a glimpse of wild love birds, baby javelina, roadrunners, rattlesnakes (yup, I'm weird and enjoy seeing them), gila monster (I have yet to see one in the wild which is crazy. If you haven't guessed it, I live in the desert in Arizona). A really great day is when I wake up early enough to go stand up paddle boarding and get to see wild horses on our lower Salt River.

One morning I watched bald eagles soar at sunrise, and a raccoon catching fish (do raccoon(s) even eat fish? Apparently, they do. The reason I'm sharing this with you, is because there is a lot of shit in this world that can bring sadness, fear, and anger. What I've found, is that happiness can be attained if you work for it, recognize it, and appreciate it. When the suck is at its absolute worst, I wake up and exercise. My mind shifts off of the suck and onto the beauty around me; the gratitude for what my body is allowing me to do. Happiness is attained if you go after it. It takes practice and it is worth it.

Once again:

There is a lot of shit in this world that can bring sadness, fear, and anger. What I've found, is that happiness can be attained if you work for it, recognize it, and appreciate it. When the suck is at its absolute worst, I wake up and exercise. My mind shifts off of the suck and onto the beauty around me; the gratitude for what my body is allowing me to do. Happiness is attained if you go after it.

So go after it!

Sometimes you can't avoid the suck, but you sure can face it by pushing through it and believing you can find happiness on the other side of it.

The first chemo round was surprisingly uneventful. I had been told that I would need someone to drive me to/from each chemo round, as in the past, I would be pumped full of heavy doses of Benadryl, anti-nausea medication, and steroids. However, as I learned very quickly, I would be just fine. I could drive myself in the future. I was also told that I should expect each round to be about four hours, however it really only takes two. The philosophy of "it'll be alright" sure was working.

The nurses were surprised to learn that I had not been offered a tour of the facility nor had I been told that I had to take a class on what to expect with chemo. It seems there were a few balls dropped. I'll be honest, after having been through chemo before and after freaking out from reading blog posts on what to expect with these types of chemo, I'm grateful that I missed the tour and the class.

The Pertruzamab was very uneventful. The Gemcitabime, which I now call "Jim Beam" was quite painful. It burns and tears up the lining of your vein and you definitely feel it going in. Fortunately, it only lasted 30 minutes and I could put my mind somewhere else to handle it. Afterwards, I felt a little tired, but not horrible. I did not feel nauseous until several days later and then decided to take the anti-nausea medication they had prescribed

The first day, I opted to rest, but that was because I had been up since 4am to ride my bike 20 miles before my 7:45AM appointment. So, it was an early start and my nerves were pretty shot.

Day two I jumped on my mountain bike and was really grateful to feel pretty normal other than a mild headache and sort of minor hangover feeling.

The first day of chemo, I had tossed out to my network a video where I stated my mindset. Instead of letting folks just wake up and pray for me, I asked them to be a little bit more out of their comfort zones, to go outside and get inspired with some activity. Remember we talked about this having happened so successfully once before. I thought I'd try it again. It worked! I received hundreds of photos of people doing everything from climbing trees, to running, biking, kayaking, camping in the middle of a baseball field to planting gardens. Every picture that rolled in made my heart soar. All of these people were doing something great for their souls because I asked them to! Well, since this challenge went so well, I had formed a Facebook group called "Get Outside Get Inspired" and asked people to join me in stating their own challenge (exercise for 30, 60, 90 days straight). I stated my challenge would be to exercise every day until I finished chemo and radiation. This was not that easy to do and I explained that exercise can take many forms and it's simply about being more active than you would normally be so if you are flying a lot in a day maybe you walk the airport instead of sitting at your gate waiting to board, etc.

The first week of chemo was filled with great activities and lots of fun BBQ's for friends and family. I took my girls outside to swim, to ride their bikes, and even to do stand-up paddle boarding for the first time. Minus a couple of nauseous moments and a few headaches and need for a nap here or there, I would say it was a successful start. I continued to say "It'll be alright".

Chemo round number 2 was also uneventful. In fact, I found myself not needing naps and really feeling pretty normal. Decided to stay away from alcohol, because even a half a drink would lead to nausea. Prior to this round of chemo, I had an epiphany after speaking with a good friend who had colitis. The reality is that most people live with an ailment every day of their life… for some its diabetes and for others it is asthma and for me it just happens to be cancer. Any health-related issue can be life threatening and can be emotionally and physically draining. The way you choose to work with your situation makes such an impact on how resilient you can be. I've chosen to use my health situation to positively impact the people and the world around me so that we create a snowball of positive energy surrounding the dreaded topic of cancer. In fact, as I learned recently, there are countries and cultures where even talking about cancer is taboo. It's time to change that situation and make it comfortable for people to ask questions and to thrive.

After the 2nd round of chemo, each new one brought challenges. My veins became harder and harder to access and less and less cooperative. It was incredibly painful to sit through multiple attempts at accessing veins. By the 6th round I started asking questions to be sure that I had an experienced nurse who was feeling confident that day. Confidence and body posture matter. If I sensed mediocrity, then I'd simply ask for someone else because I was no longer in the mood to be "practiced" on. Just like in the past, counting down and making it to the finish line became my focus.

CHAPTER 5 – A WARRIOR'S MINDSET

"Above all, be the heroine of your life, not the victim"
– Nora Ephron

I've been called a warrior. This is a term that seemed a bit extreme to me at the time but I've come to realize it is an appropriate term. I'd probably modify it to warrior princess but you get the idea. When we think about a warrior, typically the first thing that comes to mind is someone battling in the military. My definition of a warrior today is anyone who can show consistency in their ability to show up during the toughest obstacles in life. It is someone capable of developing mental toughness. The warrior mindset is the ability to combine psychological and physical strength. I would say that fighting forward through life's big speed bumps require just that. Although there have been many times where I was a flight risk in my own mind and felt fearful or unable to move forward, I did. I showed up every day through the sludge of radiation; every day and through the shit storm of chemo; and through chemo every three weeks for 13 months, even without knowing if any of it was working or if we were overdoing it. So, warrior it is.

Why do so many fail at just showing up consistently when it is painful, physically or emotionally or both? I'm not sure it's much more than what causes one person to achieve a New Year's resolution and so many others to fail. It is the difference between a habit and an intention. You may set the intention but follow-through is the most critical component.

Have you ever committed to meet someone or a group of people for happy hour or for a hike or even a friend who is in town and then you just didn't feel like getting off the couch, or didn't feel like going because work drained you? Did you end up showing up or do you have a flake factor? Now, I'm not talking about a time where you got sick and didn't go... that's different. During those times, I'd ask if you showed up for yourself and bowed out of showing up to take care of yourself? That in itself is hard for me to do. It's pure torture actually. And, it's still crucial and what warriors do.

Most people when asked will tell you that they brushed their teeth that morning but for most brushing your teeth isn't painful or emotional (my kids might disagree yet they still do it). This is because it's become a habit. A crucial habit – I will tell you that follow through has always been a challenge for me, because I am wired to get excited about the next big thing, or something else catches my attention. I have a genetic predisposition to want to only do that which is fun. Well, I've got news for you, visiting doctors, constantly doing bloodwork, having surgery, EKG's, MRI's, CT scans, chemo, and radiation are far from fun. They cause the toughest of individuals to wince and probably sometimes run. So, how was I able to do it? A warrior mindset that's how.

I kept thinking, "Will this one last round matter?". We have no proof that I need this much radiation or that I need this much chemo, so how about I call it "good enough"? BUT the nag inside my head said, "Um, nice try warrior princess. You're not done yet." Now when someone says, "It is one thing to fight cancer once in an epic way, but only a warrior can do it twice.", I kind of have to admit they are right. I've just never thought of myself in this way but I am programmed now with habits to be successful. I am resilient through tumultuous times. I know I could do it again and again and again. I now know the keys to successfully "showing up" in spite of the suck.

Being resilient is about finding a reason to smile every day. It can be found by connecting with another human and finding a way to give someone else a smile. The dopamine that is released when you do a kind act for another person is what leads to happiness.

When you have an opportunity to focus on one act of kindness a day, you'll see the impact of that turning into happiness in a slow drip fashion until it is a habit.

Throughout my battles, I've introspectively observed and asked myself, "Why do I show up every day to every treatment when there is no evidence that it is going to save my life?" My brain says, "Welllll, you show up every day because the absence of showing up is quitting. You my dear are wired for hard shit. So, when things get unpleasant, you show up and you warrior on; that's why". That brain of mine made no sense when running from pain and finding comfort sounded a heck of a lot better.

Think on that for a minute. Would you keep showing up? It's interesting, because that is a hard one to answer unless you've faced it. Instead, think about something hard for you to do or something that causes you anxiety and now process if you could keep doing it every three weeks or every day?

Let me give you an example that might make more sense because we've probably all been there before: You should be studying for a final exam. Without studying for it, there is a chance you will lower your GPA or possibly have to re-take the class. You have a friend inviting you to the beach for the day, an invite that doesn't come often. You opt for the beach and tell yourself that the studying can wait until tonight and you'll just have to pull an all-nighter. It's classic pain avoidance even though the pain won't go away and it will likely worsen.

Habits stack up. In fact, it's often the habits you form and do every day that will make the biggest gains. That's called discipline. It isn't about showing up once; it's about showing up Every. Single. Day.

Think about some of your basic habits, and while some of you may not have these and I'm laughing with you not at you, here are some basics:

-Brushing your teeth

-Making your bed (ok, not all of you may do this but those who do)

-Putting your clothes on

-Taking vitamins

These rituals are so routine that you probably don't have to think about them and they just happen, or you feel like you forgot to do something important right? Well, if you take notice of the habits that make the biggest impact and help you versus harm you, you can see that it isn't about doing them every once in a while. It's about doing them every single day. Sure, you can brush your teeth randomly but over time your teeth will stain and you'll have cavities.

One day while I was getting my hair colored and cut (because after chemo, I have a full head of grey hair), I sat listening to a lady tell her hair stylist how over six months of bad eating habits and deciding to enjoy all of the food around her, she gained thirty pounds. She then explained that she didn't want to buy a whole new wardrobe, so she decided it was time to form better habits and go on a diet. She's been on this diet for three months and can't understand why she has only lost two pounds. Now, while there could be a lot at play there, the reality is that it will take her shifting her mindset to a highly disciplined set of new habits every single day with no cheating to fix the situation. The habits that she fell into are now locked in as true habits. To change them is going to mean creating new rewards for the new habits, for them to stick and for her to transform into a warrior. It is absolutely doable though an incredible battle. I would argue it's just as hard as showing up for chemo or radiation every day. This is the difference in the way a warrior thinks.

A motivational speaker and author named Nir Eyal wrote a book called, *"Indistractable"* and in one of his LinkedIn posts he eloquently validated my thinking. He says that the problem with only having a vague understanding of how motivation works, is that if you're relying on wind to inflate your sails then you could be dead in the water if there isn't wind that day. He shares that motivation is the desire to escape discomfort. We must realize that discomfort isn't a bad thing and use it to leverage the less desirable behaviors that lead to outcomes we don't want to see.

The mind is unequivocally the most fascinating and powerful organ in our bodies. It has the ability to re-shape nearly every aspect of our being if the right motivation presents itself.

When you believe in yourself, you can *will* your body to do amazing feats.

Our eight-year-old daughter literally stopped being able to swallow solid food over the course of two weeks. In this time frame, she worsened. She was down to only being able to drink or swallow liquids, yogurt, ice cream, popsicles, soup broth, or pudding. She had no trauma other than her braces had recently been tightened and she had no obvious tonsil issues like tonsilitis or strep. Her tonsils were not red but seemed a little large.

At first, we thought she was faking and were annoyed with her for wasting so much food. We also thought it was a ploy to eat more ice cream, because after all, isn't that its own food group? We started to notice, however, she was coming home from school starving and said she couldn't eat the pizza or hamburgers and that got my attention. We then noticed she very much wanted to eat a piece of toast or a bowl of cheerios and avoided them. We did several experiments and then we started to panic. She was losing weight, starving, and scared. When we took her to a doctor, she was put through a round of tests to check about 60 different muscles needed for swallowing (primarily with tongue function) and found no issues existed. She did have swollen tonsils, which was likely residual inflammation from covid she had gotten over a few weeks earlier.

The doctor told her that she needed to do two things to improve her condition:

1. She needed to swallow a couple of drops of oregano oil mixed with juice 2x/day for 5 days OR until she was able to eat solid food.

2. She needed to tell her brain that she could swallow food. She told her that her tongue and throat are capable of it and she just has to force her brain to agree.

We went home and I demonstrated how to drink down the oil of oregano and juice and said that the faster you do it, the faster you'll get better. Holy crap, if you haven't done that before, give it a try...yowza! It is awful and it burns like a jalapeno kind of burn but it goes away relatively quickly. Well, after 45 minutes of crying and whining and putting it in her mouth and then spitting it out, she finally drank it.

She looked at me and said, "Mom, if I can eat some pita bread and show you that I can now swallow, I never have to swallow that awful stuff again, right? The doctor said 2x/day for 5 days OR until I can eat solid food. Do you agree?". I told her absolutely, but questioned how in the world she was going to be able to swallow solid bread suddenly and I watched her do it. It looked like it was quite an undertaking and her eyes got big when she swallowed but after 14 days, she ate solid food with no surgery, no medicine, just the power of suggestion. She proceeded to eat everything she had missed for 2 weeks. I was in awe of the intensity that had to occur for her to be motivated enough to break through her fears of swallowing just to avoid "that yucky oregano stuff". Her tonsil swelling eventually went down and her orthodontist said that her jaw had likely been impacted by the work they had done, contributing to the challenge. In the end, her mind just needed an ultimatum.

Let's shift gears and talk about what was happening at the end of this, my second battle with breast cancer. It is important, because "it" created warriors and weaknesses and fears and ultimately challenged the way that people lived. It challenged humanity. The "It" is Covid-19.

Global Disruption – (Covid-19)

January of 2020 still had our family excited about taking our girls for their 6th birthday to Innsbruck, Austria to ski. We were inconvenienced by the time and how hard it is to break away for this kind of trip after having already been "off" for the holidays. We always race mountain bikes in mid-February and days off the bike could hinder that performance. Worse yet, we could get sick from traveling and not be able to race. My mom traveled with us as she had not been to her favorite cities in Bavaria and Austria in roughly 40 years.

It is moments like these that remind me how precious life is and how grateful I am for my stubborn push for epic adventures and memories for our girls. We took this trip and became nervous as the news started elevating the fear of a global pandemic. At the end of January, it was really Wuhan, China that was in such trouble from a virus that was started by a man who ate a bat or so the story goes.

Covid - 19 is a nasty virus that will forever change the world. Its impact will be felt for decades and will change commerce, human resources, and even every day considerations like hugging.

I'll explain more on the virus in a moment. Over the holidays I remember listening to a podcast on gratitude and happiness. Dr. Tal Ben-Sherer stated that if you can think about what love language you are (let's use touch for example, which is one of my love languages) and something that matters to you deeply (in this case hugging was used as the example). Now imagine not being able to have, give, or receive that one thing for one month. If you're unfamiliar with The Five Love Languages, then do look it up, because it is a wonderful book on how people give and receive love.

So how would that impact you? What amount of gratitude would you have from that point forward for each time you experience a hug? At the time, the question and example made me laugh, because I thought it was absurd. Why would I ever have to go a month without hugging other people? Well, my worst nightmare happened. In place of hugs, people simply moved to smiles which were hard to see behind masks or head nods and maybe if you were lucky, you got an elbow bump.

We traveled home from Austria and surrounded by people coughing for nearly 18 hours straight and were convinced that we would get sick. We did, but fortunately for us it was just a basic cold. We were able to do my favorite race of the year and absolutely kick butt doing it. I have mentioned before, the 24 Hours of Old Pueblo put on by Epic Rides. My husband and I competed with dear friends, two who got me into mountain biking (from Alaska and from Prescott), my husband, and the first friend we made when we moved to Phoenix seven years earlier. All five of us worked tirelessly together and had no crashes, no mechanicals, and all turned out our fastest laps to land on the podium in a hard-fought battle for 5th place. I cherish that memory now more than ever, because it was the last race of that year. Every single race scheduled for the rest of 2020 was canceled because of the virus.

If you had told me that in addition to no hugging there would be no racing, I'd again have told you that it was absurd. And, yet, there we were working on finding ways to keep ourselves motivated to stay in race shape. Gratitude fills my heart, because I don't believe I will ever take those two things for granted again.

Now let's share a little bit about the shit show that commenced after that race, because it tested even me; a warrior.

I knew that after the race was over, I'd be starting four weeks of going into a hyperbaric chamber to prepare me for surgery in early April. The hyperbaric chamber is known to heal amputees, burn victims, and radiation patients and to create new blood vessels where they've been destroyed. Unfortunately, for me, it created severe anxiety because of not only how many hours a day it would tie me up, but also because I'd be confined in a chamber for several hours. So, in exploring the anxiety, my husband was right, it really was all about having no control over anything going on. The chamber is like a very small airplane cockpit with enough seats for about 8-10 passengers and they call each round a "dive", because you're essentially scuba diving down to a depth where the oxygen can be most impactful.

The surgery I was preparing for was to do some reconstruction on my chest. We were going to replace the destroyed implant on my right side. We would replace the left side and do some modifications, because my implants were sitting in very different places on my body…one up high and one where it should be. This all happened as a result of radiation. It was not only uncomfortable and looked weird, but it also had created imbalances in my back, hips, knees and an overall misalignment.

So, the chamber started on the same day as our girls' spring break, which made it extra challenging to make sure we had coverage for watching them. On top of all of that the corona virus had started to really amp up and it was no longer just China impacted. Our President, Donald Trump, had put some temperature testing in place at some airports for fevers and really was just testing anyone coming in from China, which made no sense to me. I was thinking that it could be anyone at that point coming from anywhere, but what did I know. Well, apparently, I knew more than I realized.

OH! I might have forgotten to mention, this was also my first week of officially becoming President for Lodging Dynamic Hospitality Group and running a company of 24-hotels and roughly 800-employees. From a work standpoint, I was starting to think that it might be time to think about tightening up our staffing, putting a hiring freeze on, and cutting all travel. By Tuesday (a day later) that is precisely what I did.

So, back to this hyperbaric chamber. First of all, on the Friday before the chamber was to begin, I had still not been scheduled and was at wits end with the hospital who said they were still waiting on insurance paperwork but that they knew I'd be starting on Monday and they just didn't know what time. Well, I'm the kind of person who doesn't do well with incompetence and even worse deplorable operations processes. I asked the scheduler, whom I had been calling for three weeks now, if she had seen this before and she told me oh yes, it happens all the time. Of course, my next question really wasn't meant for her but it came tumbling out anyway, "If this happens all the time, then shouldn't a new process be put in place so that you're giving the patient more than the day or one day's notice to show up for a three-hour process and a big chunk out of their day every day for 4-5 more weeks?". She of course had no answer.

I asked her if I could please be put on the schedule so I could plan for someone to watch my kids for that 4-hour chunk of time M-F of the upcoming week, because they are on spring break and not in school. She said she couldn't help me. I tried another approach. I said, "Ok, so should I get put on the schedule for Monday, what time would you say that I would be there if you had to take your best guess at it?" She said it could be anytime between 7:45am-12:30pm for my start time and that I'd be finished anywhere between 11am and 3pm. Right about that point, I lost my shit. I asked to speak to a supervisor. Now I'm not proud of who I become when I am faced with someone who simply cannot understand another human's pain points or fears. It's not pretty. She said she didn't have a supervisor. I said, "I don't know or care what the person's title is, I want to speak with whoever is your boss or is capable of helping me." She quickly said, "oh she's not available, but I will have her call you.". I retorted with "I doubt that.". Within 2 minutes, I had a phone call back from the Burn Unit Manager and she was highly apologetic. She understood completely and said there was a mix up in my paperwork and she quickly helped answer all of my questions and get me on the schedule. She talked through what to expect and assured me that new processes would be implemented to try to make it less challenging for others. She added to be fair, most of their patients are retirees with grown children. I had a feeling this was the case.

Talk about stressful. Yes, I juggle a lot with kids and work and now medical but, I've been doing that quite well to this point for roughly five years, so this little process wasn't going to derail me. I might have chugged down a good whiskey shot after that call and then found a reason to laugh.

OK, now here's something to laugh about. That darn chamber. I'm a scuba diver. I've been through MRI's, PET scans, CT scans (all of which put you through a tight space). I've been strapped down to a radiation table (again you can't move), but this chamber was getting to me. So, when I showed up, the regulars could tell it was my first time and they told me to put on some shoe covers and just wait my turn for blood pressure and temperature check and then do one last restroom break before going in.

A nice but very precise man came to chat with me and talk me through it all. He told me I needed to go wash off lotions and make up, take off my earrings, and that moving forward he would appreciate it if I didn't show up with those on. I wasn't to use any hair products (ok, right now you can laugh, because what I heard was bla bla bla and in my head I was thinking, "Dude, you have no need for hair products, have you seen how curly this hair is? If you think for a minute, I'm not using hair products then you're mistaken and if it was really a big deal, someone would have told me that prior to my coming here, so do your talk, but I'm still using hair products so you don't have a frizz fest on your hands.". I needed to make sure that my clothes had cotton in them all (no silk or polyester; essentially no synthetics). I went to the restroom and did what I was asked but then I checked my clothes and sure enough, I had cut the label out of my pants. I had no idea what they were made out of but they were spandex so I was pretty sure they weren't cotton. They made me change into nurse scrubs, which was fine.

The funny thing is that militant man, named Eric, turned out to be one of my favorite people and we ended up camping and mountain biking together several times. OK, but let's stick with how this chamber works.

Now as you go into the chamber, you duck and then go sit in your seat. You can't take anything in with you except paper and pen and a book. They ask everyone if they are good with whatever movie they will be playing and then they put a very tight plastic ring around your neck, which immediately made me squirm. They lock you in with a dive master, and in this case, Eric, started talking with me to warn me to chew gum and sip on water for the first 10-15 minutes while we go down to the depth we were going down to and to keep clearing my ears like I do when I'm scuba diving. It was easy. Then when we got to where we were going, he put a plastic bag over my head that is hooked up to tubes to let oxygen flow in and to allow me to breath out. Yes, it sounds awful and have you ever tried reading, writing, or talking through a plastic bag? It's absolutely ridiculous. I chose not to have headphones, because I was told the sound quality for the movie would not be good anyway. On a side note, I may have been in my late 40s but I was the youngest by about 20 years in those initial chamber dives.

Now you'll probably laugh at this but these folks seemed to all be able to fall asleep in the chamber. I was the one weirdo in there tapping my foot and counting every minute until it was time to get out. It was seriously the longest 2-2.5 hours of my life day after day after day. OK, this is dramatic and yes, I promise it's not painful and it's fully a mental game. I'm just not wired to sit still and chill out for a combined total of 4 hours of time every day for 5 days in a week for weeks on end. My mind starts adding up how much of my time could be spent doing epic stuff and it makes me uneasy. "Wasting time" isn't something I'm keen on, and this surely has huge benefits, but it's hard to see them or feel them so it's hard to do it. Now as you know by now, my philosophy is #justshowup and it's better than many others would do. So, I committed.

I offer you something to breathe in (yes, pun intended) to allow you a chuckle:

I once heard this in a yoga session-

My brain and heart divorced a decade ago; over who was to blame for how big of a mess I've become. Eventually, they couldn't be in the same room with each other. Now my head and my heart share custody of me. I stay with my brain during the week and my heart gets me on weekends. They never speak to one another. Instead, they give me the same note to pass to each other every week: 'This is all your fault"

On Sundays my heart complains about how my head has let me down in the past. On Wednesday my head lists all of the times my heart has screwed things up for me in the future. So, lately, I've been spending a lot of time with my gut. My gut serves as my unofficial therapist. Most nights, I sneak out the window in my rib cage and slide down my spine and collapse on my gut's plush leather chair that's always open for me.

Last evening my gut asked me if I was having a hard time being caught between my heart and my head and I nodded. I said, my heart is always sad about something that happened yesterday while my head is always worried about something that may happen tomorrow." My gut squeezed my hand and said, "In that case you should go and stay with your lungs for a while." I was confused. My gut said, "If you are exhausted about your heart's obsession with the fixed past and your mind's focus on the uncertain future; your lungs are the perfect place for you. There is no yesterday in your lungs. There is no tomorrow there either. There is only now. There is only inhale."

I hope you can breathe out whatever ails you and breath in positivity, optimism, and joy. It's there if you'll just make some room.

Every day in a warrior's life has to be inspiring. It has to have its reward from the hard work and the pain. There is no sense in saving it up for milestones, because warriors don't live assuming they'll make those milestones. They live for today; this day. So, infuse a little spark or a little guilty pleasure into each day.

The first fight with cancer was the hardest thing I had ever done – period; exclamation point. I had said, "I will never do that again!". Of course, that jinxed me and I sure as heck did do it all over again. The second battle with breast cancer was the hardest thing I'd ever done – period; exclamation point! And, guess what, I could fight again, and again, and again; if only it worked that way. I had hoped that I would not have to fight a third time because I was told that I was now on my reserve parachute. Ha ha. Well, fight a third time I am. I know now I will fight every day that I have left on this planet.

As I told you earlier, what I kept hearing throughout the second journey is "You are a warrior". I never saw myself as a warrior, so this didn't set right with me. But I started to realize why everywhere I turned someone was saying it.

I'm sure you have already figured it out, but before I tell you what one singular thing makes for a warrior, I should share an interesting statement that has stuck with me ever since the start to fighting cancer began.

My first oncologist said to me, "60% of my patients don't show up for chemo". 60%!

Wait what? I was dumbfounded. Why would they not show up? How is that even possible? Don't they want to live? She explained to me that it isn't that easy. Chemo is hard. Nearly half of that 60% don't even make it to the first round of chemo. Then she has better stats for rounds 2 & 3 and then severe drop offs again of people dropping out. She explained it's hard to show up for the hard stuff time and time again.

Now, I did not scientifically validate this percentage and who knows if it's even close to accurate, but for her business and her patients it represented to me a profound resemblance to much in life. Most people drop out when it gets tough.

How often do people struggle to get out of bed, to show up to work, to show up to 4:30am workouts day in and day out? How many people do you know who are that reliable for showing up for the relatively easy stuff in life but can't be depended upon to show up for the hard stuff? This isn't some "forming a habit for 30 days" kind of thing, or is it? I've come to realize it really is. It is the habit of training your brain with the "easier" stuff that creates the habits that are sustainable for the hard stuff.

Dr. Jason Selk, author of *"Relentless Solution Focus"*, talks about the science behind it. The realities are that your brain is wired to think in terms of problems, however, the real magic happens when you put in the time to train your brain to focus on solutions quickly when faced with problems. This is not something you just will into happening; like choosing to wake up happy every day. It is something that takes training. It requires working your brain and teaching it; strengthening it to have it actively engage like this Every. Single. Day.

RSF as it's called is the difference between a warrior mindset and resilient soul and tragic or even complacent soul. Right now, I speak to audiences about how you find happiness in life and that it isn't as easy as waking up saying, "I will be happy today". It is that easy once you've trained your brain to think like this and it comes very easily to me, because I've been in training for years.

Let me give you an example. At first when I would go to chemo, I would wake up and think "Ooofta. How am I going to face 9 hours of IV drips of chemicals/toxins into my body along with throwing up and feeling like shit?!". That was the problem, wasn't it?

Well, I knew I couldn't show up to those poor nurses and the other chemo patients with that kind of attitude, so instead, I shifted to what I was excited about. My solution? I focused on the people around me who needed me to show up because they showed up for me. So, I would say to myself, "I'm excited because I get to wake up and see the sunrise this morning, go for a little run, and then I get to take donuts to the nurses, wish Nancy a Happy Birthday and find out if Chief's chemo is shrinking his tumor and if he finally proposed to the love of his life after 20 years".

Do you see the difference? It made those awful days so wonderful and I may have still thrown up, but I was winning, because I was happy and it made showing up so much easier.

So, what is that number one differentiator between a resilient person and a tragic?

Just Show Up!

This should be your mantra in life, because if you just show up, you'll be preparing yourself for battle even when you weren't expecting to go into battle per se. No one expects to get blindsided in life, so what can you be doing today to prepare? Form your habits, re-shape and train your brain, and start to show up day in and day out for the things you already believe to be hard. It might be exercise, eating healthy, coaching sessions, or journaling. I don't know what is important to you that you still procrastinate on, but whatever it is; it's time to start today with changing your mindset and creating a warrior mentality.

CHAPTER 6 - YOUR GROWTH EDGE

"Turbulence is life force. It is opportunity." Ramsey Clark

There is something I have come to understand and embrace: Pain is a requirement in life if you are human. You cannot avoid it and you cannot run from it. You have to look it square in the eyes and tell it, "You will not break me! Now bring it!".

Do not fear pain, because it is a crucial catalyst for growth and development. It is as necessary as basic nutrients. Think about it. When you are a child, you must fall down to get back up and falling down hurts. You may have to touch something hot to learn that you don't want to do that again. As you get older the types of pain shift, you will feel the loss of a loved one, the pain of rejection or the disappointment of failure.

You will also experience physical pain and often with it comes psychological pain. As pain occurs, my advice is to simply square up, feel it, nurture it, and get through it. If you address pain in this way – then you will grow. If you do not – then you will stagnate and it will fester and at some point, you'll be forced to deal with it again; only now it'll be deeper and much more difficult. Face it, observe its healing and growth powers and you'll be astounded at what you're capable of. (It takes you to the 'next level'?)

Why did we just talk about pain? Well, because it often comes in heavy waves and it's unrelenting. I am (was) meant for more – let me explain.

In April of 2021, while playing pickleball (which I am very very bad at, by the way, but it makes me smile), I lunged for a ball and felt something not quite right in my thigh or hip -I couldn't figure out if I pulled a muscle or fractured something – but immediately, I had a limp and a deep pain. With all my athletic activity I'm used to injuries so I did the basic icing it, CBD lotion, and some arnica gel to see if I could get the inflammation down. Unfortunately, nothing seemed to work. The good news was that it didn't hurt or seem to be impacted by biking. The bad news is that walking hurt a lot.

After about a month of this nonsense, I messaged my oncology care team at Mayo Clinic and told them what happened and asked if it was time to do some scans of my leg/hip or whole body anyway to be sure cancer hadn't returned. I was told that we could discuss it in our next appointment in June. I was also told that maybe I should go see my primary care doctor to start exploring orthopedic surgeons. I was disturbed by the utter waste of time it would be to chase that rabbit down that set of holes.

In my appointment I was given an A+ for keeping cancer away. Wait what? How do we know I have kept cancer away? Are we going to do any scans to be sure? I was told my bloodwork looked good and I looked healthy and that scans don't usually catch the problem anyway. Plus, they cause undo harm to the body along with undo stress. I was told once again, this limp and general deep pain in my thigh or hip were something that an orthopedic doctor should tackle.

At this point, knowing we were leaving Arizona to do a lot of biking and hiking in Park City, UT for a month, I figured, I'd just suck it up and tackle it when we returned if it was still a problem.

Park City was wonderful except for the hiking or walking parts. Those were painful but the biking was so nice and I could hobble. I could still do stand-up paddle boarding as well.

Upon returning to Arizona and school starting, our family was blessed with COVID. The girls brought it home with them on the 2nd day. They had covid for only about 2 days each. I then got it and somehow it missed my husband. I call it a blessing because it kicked off a shit storm.

Here's the punch line: Stage 4 Breast Cancer (gulp)

Yup, chew on that one for a minute. It just stopped me in my tracks. I didn't see it coming because I sure as heck have felt great.

Follow this crazy train for the cliff notes that rocked our family's world:

⇒ Covid online doc says I need to be seen in person to get an x-ray of my lungs to determine if it's bronchitis or pneumonia

⇒ the urgent care doc says my lungs are clear and I'm on the mend but oh by the way, do you have an oncologist because we see a spot on your lungs that might be cancer (big gulp!)

⇒ my annual radiologist follow-up appointment happens virtually and she immediately sends me for a CT scan of my lungs

⇒ the CT scan is inconclusive on the tiny tiny tiny dot on my lungs but shows a mass that takes one entire vertebrae of my spine

⇒ she then tells me I have cancer again but we need a Petscan to determine where it is.

⇒ Petscan is shocking

So, this entire process takes a bit of time because I had to wait for a negative covid test to get moving along. The Pet scan results are supposed to take a few days to be read and analyzed and a report written up. However, literally as I'm driving out of the parking lot after the scan, my radiologist calls. She is very upset so of course I stay calm and then she tells me it's bad. I stay calm. I take deep breaths and focus on my breathing. She says it's in my spine, hips, ribs, sacrum, and the largest is in my femur that has been causing me pain since April.

Wait what? So, no pickleball accident apparently.

I make a joke and stay calm.

I look at my hubby and his eyes say it all. This is not good. I stay calm.

I'm not sure why but I decided to ask if she thinks I can make it a couple more years on this planet. She says she hopes so and that what we are fighting for is time and that along with that time, that I am not wheelchair bound. Wow, seriously? I'm back in my "what the heck" frame of mind! The problem is that the tumor in my femur is so big it's about to break the femur. She isn't sure how it hasn't broken yet and says that we don't have any time because a broken femur will be excruciating and really cause huge setbacks in our ability to fight this fast. If she could have, she would have had me in with a surgeon on that day.

My radiologist is just an incredible human. She said she has a friend who is one of the best orthopedic surgeons in Arizona who can operate and take a biopsy of the tumor to confirm it is breast cancer and not a new kind of tumor. She can place a rod in my femur and hip to stabilize it. And she can do all of this in just a few days!

So, my head is spinning and I'm no longer calm but I've been here before. Overwhelmed, scared, and in pain. Let's face it head on.

I'm immediately placed on crutches with hopes that I can make it 4 days without the femur breaking. OK, those who know me, would know there was no way I was using those when I was so used to hobbling around without crutches. I also continued to bike. YES, I am crazy. I don't recommend following in my footsteps.

However, with this short timeline, we had to share the news with everyone fast because it was time to ask for help. I crumbled up my business that I had been working so hard to ramp up, created a list of needs for this massive undertaking, and we put it out to the universe. I didn't really even know what "it" was that we were telling everyone and honestly just had to share it as it was happening and as we were learning more.

Probably one of the hardest videos to create was a Marco Polo to tell my family and then the next hardest was doing one for everyone else on social media. It felt so impersonal but with short notice, I sure wanted them to hear it from me and to not be afraid. Well, I'd give me a C on this effort. I am not sure which was harder sharing the news and knowing it would hit quite a few people deeply or their receiving the news.

I attempted to create these videos about 10 times and each time I broke down. Finally, I pulled off one with still a bit of a tear jerker but at least in this one, you could understand what I was saying. Delivering bad news is not my strong suit and you'd think I would have become proficient by now. Not quite. I usually infuse humor to deliver the wallop in a more palatable way but some news is just not easy to cushion.

Do you know the difference between stage 4 cancer and terminal cancer? Well, I did not. I assumed they meant the same things. I learned that lots of people live with stage 4 cancer for quite a long time and that only when you've tried everything and it still keeps growing does it then turn into terminal cancer. I was working hard to share this news and educate people at the same time and honestly, most of the time I was able to hold it together, but boy when the flood gates broke, they kept breaking and the water works were fierce.

I'd be biking along and someone would ask "how ya holding up?" and bam, the tears turned into sobs. My friends let me cry on bike rides as much as I needed to. Truth is that they wanted to cry too and they did once they left me and didn't have to be strong. Everyone in the community we live in was rocked by it and fortunately pulled together to lift us up. It was an incredibly insane time and I can't keep a dry eye typing this to think about the outpouring of support that came in from financial donations to meals being made for us, from play date offers to shield the girls from all of this, to grocery shopping, and yes prayers. Everyone wanted to help and no one was really sure how to, but as I asked for help driving me to and from the insane number of appointments or asking for someone to get me out of the house or lend me a cane or walker or crutches, it just happened.

I set up a group chat so that I could share updates and so that I could ask for volunteers to help me and it helped so much. I believe there were 42 trips where I needed to be driven roughly 45 minutes each way.

Mike wasn't allowed to pay for his own coffee in our local coffee shop, Hava Java for about 3 months. The staff just nodded and said "it is on us".

So, how were we handling all of this? I'd say we were looking the pain in the face and facing it. I told Mike that if I had known I was going to put him through all of this that I would never let him marry me. We cried holding each other and both knowing that our girls are still so young and that they really need the best of both of us for as long as possible. Mike as always said, "I'd still marry you even knowing I'd go through all of this." These are the moments where the pain dulls for just a moment and allows us to carry on through more of it ahead.

So, on one hand, I'm thinking about a quote by James Howe, "Life's short and there will always be dirty dishes, so let's dance." And on the other hand, I'm literally consumed with doctors' appointments, physical therapy, and attempting to formulate a game plan for a strategy that has yet to be written.

Everything was uncertain and scary and with all of it, I was determined to protect my magic. I simply took one day at a time and truly savored every moment and realized this is a gift to allow me to be even more present than before and to realize again that if you want to be happy you must practice it every single day.

When faced with adversity promise yourself you too will protect your magic!

Now, I'm not going to lie, I was and still am angry as I type this, because, this could have been caught much earlier. I was angry that I was overlooked. I was angry I let myself be overlooked. I decided that although my oncologist had an amazing reputation, oodles of years of experience, and incredible results, he clearly had gotten sloppy. I was certain I needed more opinions.

That was a long arduous process. Just to get appointments to discuss my case took major favors to be called in. I wanted opinions on strategy from senior doctors and from new doctors as long as they were cutting edge. Each opinion I got came back with what I expected: A need to do a hard-core chemo mixed with what I call "chemo light" which is Herceptin and Perjetta or Pertuzemab.

Of course, my incredible naturopathic doctor, Dr. Daniel Rubin was along for this ride and by my side as always.

He knows me well and wanted to put me back in charge of at least part of the outcome, so he suggested I start doing treatments called ozone therapy, which he likened to having bouncers in your club to kick out the trouble maker cells which we call circulating tumor cells. The ozone seeks out these tumor cells and stops them from being able to set up shop in other organs or locations.

We did a week of radiation to my leg/hip once it healed to try to turn those tumors into ash in my bones.

And, just like with my second battle, I began to seek out the best way to eat and live to try to fight with food. Recently there had been studies linking certain blood types to having better results on a vegan, plant-based diet (and no sugar) or on keto, which I had success with before though it was a lot of work. Dr. Rubin's assessment was that with my being A+ blood type, I would do better on a plant-based diet. Well, talk about overwhelming! Oh my gosh so many people had gone plant based, lots of podcasts had been created on planet-based lifestyles and benefits of it and a tremendous number of cookbooks. It still felt daunting. I loved bacon and eggs and sushi and cheese, oh my gosh no cheese?! Eek!

Well, to just get me started, an incredible friend gave me her juicer and brought over lemons, celery, cucumbers, green apples and ginger and taught me how to start by at least having a juice a day. Within a few days I felt more energetic. Thank you, Cathy,…you are a real treasure.

Additionally, one day when I hobbled to the local bike shop to wait for my husband and fellow cyclists to finish their ride and come for coffee, I noticed a runner I'd known looking uncomfortable but clearly wanting to talk. He finally admitted he didn't know what to say to me, what not to say, or even what to ask. Just seeing me there made him uncomfortable. I soon began to realize this happening a lot. So, I comforted him and told him that there is nothing he can say or do that would offend me. Ask anything and in particular ask questions about the now.

He asked a great question that led to a breakthrough! He asked me what I struggled with the most right now. The answer was easy. How do I become vegan? His eyes lit up. He had been vegan for 2 years and loves it. I asked him to walk me through a typical day of food. What does he eat and drink? He got so excited.

We literally created a grocery list and menu for me for a couple days of ideas. We talked about the pitfalls, cravings and replacements, the upside, the challenges of being the only vegan in the house or at a dinner party. It lifted both of our spirits so much. Cory Hove, you started me down a path I never realized I'd love so much. At this point it's been 9 months and even if I didn't have cancer, I'd be eating vegan. It feels so good. It has decreased inflammation, given me energy, and kept me from experiencing some of the harder side effects that are expected with this kind of fight.

Truly this put me in charge. A side benefit is weight loss but healthy weight loss.

While I distracted myself with learning how to be vegan and physical therapy to heal from that massive surgery of placing a pin straight through my femur and hip, I was still waiting for my final meeting with my oncologist where I listened to him and then planned to fire him, because of his failure to listen to me for precious months.

In fact, I even had chemo set up and planned for the following week with another doctor.

Eventually, I did meet with my oncologist and while he is not the apologizing type, he gave me a completely different take on how we approach my surviving. He said that he's been doing this for so many years that he happens to have several patients who have successfully survived a decade already and that he believes we can win this by treating it as a marathon and not a sprint distance race. Hard chemo yet again is just going to be too damaging to my organs which have been through so much over the past eight years. He believes that by using two types of "chemo light" to keep cancer cells from replicating and communicating AND by emptying out the gas that feeds these tumors (estrogen) that we can shrivel up the tumors in my bones and keep them from spreading to other organs.

He also had a suspicion that the tiny tiny dot on my lung is not a tumor but rather something residual from radiation. He said his experience will get me through this and that he won't lose sight of me moving forward. He asked if I'd keep him as my doctor and asked what it would take to do so.

Well, he has so much more experience than the wonderful man who I was going to entrust with my life. AND, this character had kind of grown on me.

I had one ask of him. It was that he never have me meet with the woman who dismissed me and told me to go see my primary care physician. I told him that if I met with her that it would be dangerous for her because I might actually punch her in the face. He knows that I joke around a lot but this time he laughed and said he understood and then he looked into my eyes to see that, in fact, I was totally serious. He got serious and promised that I would not have to meet with her and that he had other assistants and nurses that I could meet with throughout treatment.

So, of course, now that you know me, you'll know that I like a good challenge. I would like to beat the decade or so that my doc has seen from other patients and survivors. We no longer count how many rounds of treatment that I have left, because there is no end. This may sound terrible, but honestly, it's like brushing your teeth. Do you count how many more times you'll brush your teeth in this lifetime? I think not. We don't count, we simply show up. I say we, because it is no longer just my fight. It is my family fighting and it is my friends who know when I've had my treatments and who know that I'll have a little bit of a "hangover" on the bike the next day when riding. It's a whole team who fights with me.

Hanging in our home are these two signs that pretty much sum it up - "Life is like riding a bicycle. To keep your balance, you must keep moving." – Albert Einstein

And "When in doubt, ride it out"

It took many months to get me back to walking again and riding my bike again, but the simple things took even longer. I kept watching my kids easily sit on the floor and I longed for that and wondered if I would ever be able to do that again and what I found is that if you try every day then yes, you can. It took 6 months but now I can plop down on my knees on the floor and sit again. Getting up is a little wonky, I have a limp and a completely numb right foot all day long every day, but these things should improve over time if I keep seeking healing and strength.

This absolutely epic life is made possible by my ability to be resilient. Yes, I have curated this epic life and I've been blessed by pain to create a reason for intense learning. This is not a static process. It is going to require me to never let off the gas in this fight.

So far, the PET scans show that we are winning. The cancer appears to have shriveled up into the dead coral we were hoping to see and so far, hasn't taken up residence in any other organs. So, we stay on strategy. What I suspect is that the lack of estrogen and the Her2 "chemo light" combo is keeping those tumors dead and likely the no sugar and plant-based diet is making it so that the side effects that might be present are so diminished that I don't really even have any side effects. Possibly it is making my body uninhabitable by tumors. At some point we may have to adjust the strategy or it may stop working, but until that time, I'm going to keep fighting.

I'm not going to diminish the fears that existed for the shots that put me into menopause or the medication that I take daily (anastrazole) to keep the additional estrogens out. My anxiety for this whole-body change was intense x100. In fact, the first few weeks, my notes on side effects were pages long. However, as time passed, by the time I met with my doctor for another round of treatments, I had almost nothing to tackle with him. He instead asked me about side effects that are nearly always present in 98% of his patients. These include joint pain, spine pain, depression, foggy brain, hot flashes, night sweats, dry irritated skin, and my answer to all of it is "nope". Night sweats and hot flashes truly only happen if I've had sugar. He was baffled and said this is all fantastic and the blood work showed that I was in fact deep into menopause. We both believe the lack of side effects have been a result of the plant-based, no sugar diet.

It's still too early to truly declare a victory but at this point, we are 9 months into treatments and all is going smoothly.

Yes, I'm back on my bike and stand-up paddle board and in fact, I have even gone snorkeling with whale sharks and snow skiing in powder. I'm definitely lowering my intensity in all things cardio to protect my heart and hopefully to keep it stronger by not exceeding 90-minutes a day of cardio workouts. I'm also cautious enough to try to protect my body from bone breaks for another 6-9 months while we work with a shot to push calcium to my bones since everything, we have me on is trying to create fragile bones. And, yes, mountain biking, snow skiing, SUP, and racing all come with risks but I'm back to living like I'm living and not living like I'm dying and that feels great.

As Emma Stone said, "You live once and life is wonderful so eat the damned red velvet cupcake."…only my velvet cake is going to be made with SWERVE sugar instead of real sugar ha ha.

CHAPTER 7 – SHINE BRIGHT

"In spite of my scars, I'm tickled to death with life!"
– Eugene O'Neill

L et's talk for a moment about what it takes to truly show up, because in fact, you now know it isn't that easy. If it were that easy and intention was all that was needed then wouldn't more people achieve their New Year's resolutions?

So, what makes people successful? I believe there are three things:

1. Curate Your Own Happiness

2. Exercise

3. Create Boundaries

Curate Your Own Happiness

On the surface this sounds easy. Just be happy. I know right? It's not that easy. Here are a few life hacks that I believe make curating your own happiness absolutely achievable, but it'll require some introspective time.

First of all, you have to be mindful of what brings you joy and what doesn't. I recommend making a log or journaling for a couple of days. Make note of the things that bring you peace or joy and notice the things that create anxiety or depression. Next up, you've got to cognitively choose to cut the things that do not bring you joy. OK, I know you can't cut everything, but you can creatively approach those things or even outsource them. For instance, I don't enjoy laundry, so instead of doing laundry daily, I've found that doing it twice a week and incorporating the help of my family, allows us to get it done faster. My approach has changed.

Cut anything that doesn't bring you joy

If you read my first book, you'll know that I cut all sorts of things that didn't bring me utter joy. When was the last time you said, "Oh ya, I want to be inspired this morning, so I'm going to turn on the news!"? Probably never! So, I cut it and stopped watching or listening to the news each day and I found a huge shift in my PMA (Positive Mental Attitude). In eight years, I can honestly say that I haven't missed anything. You'll find out about anything earth shattering anyway.

The hardest things to cut are people. I cut a variety of social media apps that created frustrations and I also, sadly, cut people. If anyone looked at me like I was dying then they were out. If they hadn't reached out or commented on anything in my posts then they were cut. Or if they posted very sad or politically charged issues then they were gone as well. It left room for the core people who I knew would want true authentic updates.

The things that I chose to replace those cuts with were very positive. I infused morning dancing into my routine; generally, when I'm making my coffee. I also infused learning how to be my own barista and try out different flavors and textures of lattes. Learning is so great for uplifting the soul.

Another way to curate your own happiness is to revisit how you approach vacations. An epiphany occurred to me while "people watching". I saw that many people create so much stress leading up to a vacation that it's challenging for them to relax for several days. They may struggle to disconnect at all. And any good that comes from the vacation is quickly lost in the stress of working tirelessly on their return to get caught up. Thus, I believe in infusing a mini-vacation into every day.

Infuse a mini-vacation in every day

If you infuse a mini-vacation into every day then you've learned the art of sustained energy management. Andy Warhol said, "You need to let the little things that would ordinarily bore you suddenly thrill you." And I agree with that but with a little twist. Change it up. You see by just making a small change, your perspective and reward can change as well. Choose a different ice cream flavor or a different shop. Take a different route to a routine place.

I'm wired to need energy bites in each day. I call them energy bites and you might just call them workouts, but without them, my energy fades and I start to feel like I should just stay on a couch or take a nap.

As a side note, I don't nap very well and that isn't a good thing. Naps are so powerful. I have a hard time settling my brain enough to take a nap but when I do, wow, it makes a huge difference in my energy. I am the queen of power napping (10 minutes of hard rest can carry me through the rest of a day and yes, I realize that sounds like a teaser for most but truly it's all I need).

Anyway, these energy breaks and naps are important and can sometimes be your mini vacation in the day. Sometimes I walk with my kids or jump on a bike with them for a short distance or maybe I just crank up some music for one song and dance or I walk to the mailbox.

My suggestion is to brainstorm a list of things that would give you joy to break up your day and give you energy at the same time. What are some things that would make you giggle or even go against the grain or social norms? If you brainstorm it now, it's sort of your pick list or bucket list of "mini-vacation moments".

One of the things I have done on occasion is to take my girls into school 30 minutes late so we could bike to breakfast and enjoy breakfast together and then we bike to school. They miss out on almost nothing plus they gain so much from it and it makes me giggle. Another example is that I play pickleball with friends once a week or I meet my husband for lunch (for us that is a great energizer because we almost never get breaks when we are both working; much less time together without kiddos. It is for sure a mini-vacation).

Lastly, when it comes to curating your own happiness, never under value the power of doing something for other people. Volunteerism or random acts of kindness once a day can immensely increase your smile lines. Much like the list of mini-vacation ideas, I would suggest a list of kindness ideas you can quickly grab from when you need a pick me up each day. These should be fast and they don't have to cost you any money. Maybe it's calling someone you haven't spoken with in a while, maybe it's buying someone a coffee as you buy your own, or maybe it's picking up a meal or making one for someone moving, so they don't have to even find their dishes to cook in for a night or two. There are so many things that you can do on the fly for another human being that truly green up the human spirit. I dare you to try and carry a frown when you do this. It is nearly impossible.

Do random acts of kindness or volunteerism every day

Have you ever noticed the smile that happens when genuine random acts of kindness are done? Have you ever thought about how good you feel for creating that response in another human being? Have you ever given selflessly of your time to help others? If you do not know this feeling yet or have never really done this before, try it. It can be like the endorphins that are released with exercise. A small act can have a huge positive effect, momentarily causing your own physical or emotional pain to disappear. I can tell you right now, that just as euphoric as you feel while exercising, this somewhat small thing, creates huge positive chemicals to be released and it momentarily causes your own pain whether physical or emotional to disappear.

Now how do you even get started? At first it may take another brainstorming session and some research but then it will start to become part of your normal operating system. I know that it is now part of mine, because I've bought other people their breakfast at Starbucks or ice cream cones/gelatos often enough now that my girls have started saying, "I wonder who we are treating today?". ☺ That makes my heart happy.

Those things cost money, but there are plenty of things that do not that can make a huge difference. If you are going to the grocery store, could you offer to pick up groceries for a neighbor? Do you have talents where you could go entertain or visit with some residents of a retirement center? How about volunteering to read a story to neighborhood kids?

There are simply acts of kindness all around if you just look up and observe the opportunities. While flying with my girls and having my hands quite full with luggage and breakfast, and honestly, two not so helpful eight-year-olds on this particular day, an incredible moment happened. There were a group of young adults traveling together and they were truly connecting with one another. They weren't immersed in technology, which gave me a smile. One of them looked up and said, "Here take my spot and let me help you with all of that." You see there were no seats available at one of the restaurants and no obvious place to stand to wait for food to go.

Wow, just wow. I think I accidentally audibly exclaimed "Oh wow, that is so kind!". He beamed and I beamed and we both wished one another a great day. It stuck with me and I hope it stuck with him because that small act of kindness in the moment when I needed it most was more than welcomed and so appreciated.

Could you water your neighbors' plants or bring in their trash can? I would say I am grateful my parents engraining this in us at a young age. For as long as I can remember growing up, we had a foreign exchange student living with us. We spent many days volunteering at our local museum and even to this day, my mom hosts tea parties for the widowed 80+ year olds in her community about once a quarter.

Whatever you choose, start today. Try it. We spend so much time in this world doing what we "need" to do. I would offer that if you pause for a moment and even took 30 seconds to grab the door for someone, you'll start to feel an uplift that I call my smiling heart. It's just a feeling of genuine happiness.

Exercise

For those who know me, you'll be tickled to learn that I have actually scaled back on exercise when I began this third battle with cancer. We'll talk about why I scaled back in a moment, but first let's talk about why exercise is so important and what exercise is and what it is not.

Exercise is probably the first thing that every doctor, including psychologists, will ask about when they talk about strategies for success. It doesn't matter what ails you. Ultimately, to combat pain, fatigue, depression, anxiety, heart problems, cancer, high blood pressure, or anything else I have forgotten, exercise is one of the most powerful solutions.

Once you discover the incredible benefits of exercise, the challenge is to incorporate it into your daily operating system. Most humans are wired to want to see results and receive a reward over and over again so that eventually just doing the exercise is tied to a feeling that is positive and even craved. Can you imagine that? You craving exercise? Well, it's possible. Stick with me for a minute.

What is exercise? Do you need to ride a bike or run every day? Nope. If you happen to enjoy that, then do it, but it isn't a requirement. However, I believe you need to exercise your brain and your body in some fashion every day.

Let's start with the body and then move to the brain.

Exercise is physical movement and I subscribe to the positive impact of exercising every day. Nope, not a few days a week but every day. I've had people tell me that my movement or outdoor challenges of exercising every day for a month have been too intimidating to even attempt. I've heard people say that the idea of exercise every day is overwhelming and unattainable. OK, fine. I feel you on this one. I remember hearing that I'd need to do radiation for 35 days with only weekend breaks and that was overwhelming. Tying the experience to something positive helped me to achieve it. Before you get started, create a reward mechanism. If you need more ideas here, then reach out to me.

Ideally exercise is one hour every day, but if that sounds ridiculous then aim for 30 minutes every day. The intensity is yours for the choosing. If you haven't read my first book then you might not know that I was a normal lazy teenager. In high school when the PE teacher wasn't looking, I'd walk. I found ways to get out of most exercise and unless it was swimming or dance/cheer I didn't want any part of it. Finally in my late 20's, I decided I wanted to do a triathlon. I needed to learn how to run. Yes, that sounds silly but I didn't know how to run.

I started off walking each day for an hour and I was getting bored. Pretty quickly, I decided that jog-walking would allow me to see more of the trail. I began jog-walking for an hour. Before not too long, I decided I could see even more so I started running for 2 minutes then walking for 5 minutes. I did that rotation for an hour. I then moved up to flip-flopping that and low and behold, one day I actually ran a whole 3 miles straight. It took this kind of building up to get me to a place where I would celebrate after each run and each run was pretty much every day for an hour.

Some people say, "...but don't you need a rest day?". Well, sure you do, if you're a professional athlete bringing intensity every day. If you're a basic human, then nope no rest day needed, because you get to "rest" 23 hours in a day as it is!

Movement should be done every day for 30-60 minutes a day

You will want to brainstorm on the kind of movement you want to incorporate. I need to work in more non-cycling related movement, because variety is important for strengthening all muscle groups throughout your body. Here are some of the movements that I enjoy: pickleball, stand up paddle boarding, walking, hiking, skiing, snow shoeing, rock climbing, swimming, and yoga. I still want to try my hand at learning silks or aerial yoga or Pilates but there is just not enough time in a day so I darn well better be around a lot longer so I can try more things!

There is such a thing as too much exercise. I never knew this! One of our friends goes to a world-famous cardiologist in Kansas City. Apparently, he has done tremendous research on athlete hearts and he has found that athletes who exercise more than 60 minutes a day at peak performance and intensity, form thicker walls around their heart, so it acts like and looks like a heart of a lethargic person, no matter their shape or size. It makes sense to me because our circle of friends are all super athletes and many have heart challenges. What I mean by that, is that they have enlarged hearts or get heart flutters like SVT (supraventricular tachycardia) or Afib (atrial fibrillation).

Check this out. My quarterly echocardiograms all showed the same sort of wall thickness until I had one done when I couldn't exercise due to *that* metal rod being hammered into my femur to keep the bone from collapsing. The echo was needed to be sure my heart could handle my starting chemo again. I wanted to know how the results compared with previous echos, since hobbling walks had been most of my exercise. While not a perfect experiment because I had gone vegan and cut sugar for a month, the test showed my heart actually in better shape than ever before.

I know, some of you are thinking, "Well you're proving that not exercising is good for me, so I'm just going to stick with it." Ha ha. NOPE. The reality is that because I had been in such great shape going into these battles and during them, I had a body ready for war. You simply can't get ready for war and come out a survivor if you are an occasional exerciser.

It would be like someone saying, "So hey, I am doing a marathon tomorrow, what should I use for fuel.". Uhhhhh, nothing you do for fuel is going to work unless you train using your fuel plan for many weeks or even months before. It's just like runners who know that you never run a marathon in new shoes. You need time to break them in and get used to each other. ☺

OK, so let's say you've chosen what exercise you're going to incorporate, you've chosen your time of day, and how long you plan to exercise along with what kind of reward awaits you after each session. You're pretty much ready to get started. Don't think about the days ahead. That will feel daunting. A girlfriend and I say that the only way you can eat an elephant is one bite at a time. You see, for most, exercise sounds as appetizing as eating an elephant. If you have to do it then you can but you can't think about the whole elephant. You can only think about one bite. If you take one bite at a time what you'll find is that one day you look up and that elephant is almost gone!

Eat an elephant one bite at a time – for goodness sakes don't look at the size of the elephant or your mind will defeat you.

Now to be truly successful, you'll need the buddy system. Movement can be done alone, however, I find that to be truly successful, it is best done with other people. Some of the most joyful times in life are spent with other people. Exercise doesn't become truly joyful until you have context that creates memories of laughter and joy. I know that it'll be painful for most of you but you may even grow to crave the pain. I don't mean true unhealthy pain but pain in the form of sore muscles and exhaustion. When you create some pain, it is powerful to have joy present so that pain becomes desirable rather than something to be avoided.

The power of exercising with friends is not just that it's more fun. It helps create an accountability system. When people are relying on you to show up, it is so much harder to let them down even if you would have been willing to let yourself down. Sometimes, even if you know that no one will notice you missing, just knowing that "your people" will be there, helps to get you there.

You see, on most days in Arizona, especially in the dark of winter, a 4:15am alarm or 4:30am alarm (I do a little later in the winter), goes off and although I'm way more programmed to get up than most humans on this planet, it still somehow hurts. It hurts more in the dark and cold of winter for sure. I'm pretty good at going to bed by 9-10pm in the winter but in the summer since it's light out until 9pm, I have room to improve on my bedtime. Being programmed and having a ritual or habit does help. Knowing that there is a small percentage of the population out there biking at the same time sure helps me to get up as well. There is something special about knowing that you're tougher than most, and that you're being productive and getting to see the sunrise. It is momentous.

If you ever have a hard time deciding "do I go or do I sleep longer?", just remember that the guilt of not going will hit you! Regret for not showing up is a powerful motivator. If you have no guilt then you simply haven't reached warrior status.

So, you might be thinking, "But I don't have time in the morning to exercise." In most cases, I'm going to tell you that is an excuse. Once when we were being picked up at 7am for a flight, I had to set my alarm for 3:45am. This was to allow me to be on my bike by 4:30 and to be in the shower by 6am. Did it hurt? Yup. Did I care? Nope. #justshowup

Also, morning is when you have the most powerful flow of testosterone and it can set your intention for the day. (Setting your intention is just a way of saying you create a positive goal for yourself) So, if you only have 30 minutes in the morning then take it and make it happen. I love to exercise for 90+ minutes in the morning and then afternoon workouts are just a bonus. My favorite is tossing in our weekly Wednesday pickleball rounds with our buddies or an evening or night time stand up paddle board session. Sometimes I'm lucky enough to get in biking, SUP, and pickleball all in a day-those are the really great days. It doesn't matter what your movement is, but get up and move. I'm not sure how it impacts you, but it lights my soul on fire and causes an incredible flow of energy and brain power. My brain literally lights up with intensity and excitement. The floodgates of ideas and clarity of direction on just about every topic is unlocked.

The science behind this can be found by reading either *Relentless Solution Focus* by Dr. Jason Selk or by reading *The Power of Fun* by Catherine Price. Both spent tremendous amounts of time researching why movement is important and the benefits of doing it. Price is known to call it "flow". Not all exercise is created equal, however, by being truly present while doing it, you'll see the benefits. Don't just go through the motions and check out but rather be totally present with the people you are with or with an instructor or even with yourself and how you're feeling.

Sometimes I feel like I'm sleep riding but I do wake up on the ride and take note of my surroundings, my body and how it's responding, how my bike is performing, and more. It takes work to stay truly present and with some effort you can train yourself to stay in the moment.

Speaking of training your brain. The brain is both a beautiful thing and a royal pain in the ass. You see the brain can cause so many challenges if you let it or it can be your most powerful tool. However, like all tools, it needs maintenance to stay useful. It also needs to be used every day to keep functioning at its best.

Proving my point, do you remember earlier I told you about our daughter, Baby A (one of our twins) who suddenly stopped eating food we would give her and we started noticing her school lunches coming home uneaten? The doctor told her to tell her brain to eat food, and visualize herself eating it. Viola, she visualized eating a bagel and after two weeks of not eating and barely drinking anything, she suddenly ate a bagel to avoid drinking an awful concoction.

Visualization is critical in accomplishing what you set out to do and reminding your brain that you absolutely can do it. This is also why it is so important to choose wisely the people you allow in your world. Surrounding yourself with people who achieve, people who exercise, and people who uplift you can remind your brain that you can accomplish what you want to accomplish.

Let me share an opposing example. We took our girls to Switzerland to ski for their 8th birthday. This was one of the most stressful trips of our lives for so many reasons but that isn't the moral of the story; just a sidebar. In the United States every ski run is labeled based on difficulty (green = easy, blue = intermediate, black = advanced). In Switzerland not only do you not have these labels; only names of runs, you also have no signs or warnings about cliff areas. While we were there, our girls literally followed us down every run we skied. They jumped off ledges, skied in deep powder, and did moguls as big as they were.

We then went to Wolf Creek ski area in Colorado after we returned from Switzerland, I found that everything was comparatively easy. Well, the girls both stopped above a black run and said, "Nope this is too hard, mom. It's a black." I took one look at that run and laughed so hard and told them that a black here is like everything they skied in Switzerland. They weren't buying it and it stopped them from doing runs they were perfectly capable of. Only the label stopped them. Now I wish we could rip down all of the labels we have in America. That statement could apply to a lot of things in our country right now. At least I was able to get them to say, "We can't do this run *yet*" versus, "We can't do this run".

If the mind is this powerful then doesn't it stand to reason you need to work it? If you haven't made time for podcasts or reading then you're probably not reading this book and not really my audience, right? Reading, introspection, meditation, growth, and learning are crucial components to working your brain. Introspective work often can be painful because it has you laboring over answers to really tough questions. And once you've determined areas to work on, you really have to put the work in to make it part of your operating system.

One of the hardest things I have ever worked on is lying still in corpse pose in yoga. It feels like eternity before we are guided to another movement. Now, I get great enjoyment out of that pose. In fact, I never realized there was a point to it. I thought, "Is this like grown up nap time?" Ha Ha. Well, now I find great value in using that time to focus on my intention and not letting my mind wander. It will forever be a challenge but one I know I can continue to perfect.

We are human so we are wired to experience fear, depression, and anxiety in our lives. Just as much as that is present, we have to work our brains to combat those things and create balance. If you practice waking up in the morning and stating three things you are grateful for and looking forward to in your day, you'll likely have a great mindset to face the world. However, it must be done every day to truly stick. Not done only randomly.

If you wake up fearful or nervous about the day ahead then likely you'll see everything that could go wrong. There is a huge difference. If you wake up happy, then you can keep that happiness factor charging you forward. Some people have to place a mirror in front of them to practice smiling or laughing and over time it just happens to show up without much effort at all. My body has been really worked over and there are a lot of aches and pains. So, to get me smiling, I start by wiggling and stretching while I brush my teeth. Then I transition to turning on a song and while I make a latte, I begin to dance. By the time I'm finished wiggling, dancing, and drinking a coffee, there is an impenetrable smile on my face. Don't worry, I'll give you some time to process this and I'll have a few introspective pages for you ahead in the appendix.

Let's just check in real quick with what it takes to "Show Up". We've talked about a need to curate your own happiness and exercise. The third component that contributes and separates the goods from the greats, is the ability to create boundaries.

Set Boundaries

Those who know me know, I don't waiver in my need for exercise. I also don't apologize for it and it will be infused in every business trip or vacation. I am not wired to sit around on Christmas morning opening presents and staying in pajamas. I would always prefer to open presents the night before and be out skiing on Christmas Day handing out candy canes to lifties (lift operators) and thanking them for working so that I can enjoy some great snow on Christmas.

My family knows this about our little family and most choose to stay away from our insanity and stick with more traditional Christmas festivities. We don't judge anyone for being traditional and we create boundaries and clearly state our unwavering intentions for how we spend our holiday. How is this possible? It's through the use of boundary setting conversations.

When it comes to setting boundaries to ensure success in showing up, I recommend you do the following:

1. Know what matters to you/what are your non-negotiables?
2. Have boundary setting conversations
3. Choose the fish to be in your fish bowl with you

You probably already know what matters to you and are non-negotiables; however, do you know them for all contexts of your life? When it came to fighting cancer, at first (eight years ago), I only knew that I wanted to be able to hold my infants as much as possible, be a solid mom, and exercise every day. I didn't know or realize that my non-negotiables would actually grow and expand. By battle number two, I also knew that time mattered to me. I wasn't willing to just give up any amount of time to my fight. I had to work to negotiate start and end times of procedures so that it didn't impinge on my time with exercise, time sitting in traffic, or time away from my kids. This sounds fairly easy but not so easy when you're dealing with an institution that is large and that has no problem wasting people's time. It meant that my doctor and I had to get aligned on basics like the fact that I don't want to be heavily medicated. I also do not want to take what they call "pre-meds", which are a litany of drugs to counteract potential side effects of the chemo drugs. They are precautionary and I figured out that I did not need them; they make me feel worse than the actual chemo infusions. These are all examples that are very specific to this aspect of my life.

What I've learned is:

1. I'm not average. I have more boundaries and requirements than the average human in most aspects of my life.

2. You probably won't accomplish what matters most to you unless you ask for it.

This #2 is true for so many aspects of your life. For instance, recently when my cousin was looking for a different job, I asked her what her wish list of requirements were for her negotiations in a job offer. Those are more important than the salary parameters. She said, "Well it would be nice to have coaching in this new leadership role, because I've never led people". Well, then ask for it was my response. She wanted more vacation time and I of course said, "ask for it". The important thing to understand is that you won't get all 'your asks' but if you know which ones are non-negotiable. So, list them all and circle the ones that are not negotiable.

Further – in negotiating for a new job I told my cousin that once you know what matters to you then the conversation is crucial. I tend to start with the punch line and jump right into stating what matters and then jump into the why behind it. Then it's time to be quiet and let the other person process it, ask questions and form their proposed path forward. To keep the upper hand, it is important for you to state why you know you can get this if you go elsewhere and that you don't need an answer right away.

For instance, in my case, my negotiables, often mean that the doctor has to go against the policies and procedures for the hospital and nothing I'm asking for is that off-the-charts weird. However, it may require them to get the rest of their team on board and that may not be able to happen immediately. Work-around and equitability are things that come into play. It may require creativity on your part and theirs and a lot of discretion.

It is easy to have these conversations when you have passion towards and behind the things that matter most to you.

Often when I'm career coaching leaders, I find that the asking and conversation are the hardest part because of fear of rejection. That is normal, however if you have back up plans and options, and can even make it collaborative by asking questions to get to where you are going, it becomes co-creation and much more powerful. Let me give you some examples:

- "Being able to work remotely so that I can be home for children when they come off the bus is important to me. How could we make this work for this role?"

- "I'd really like to cut back on my impact to the environment and decrease overall gas consumption. Are there ways that we could accomplish all of these tests, shots, and chemo rounds in a more compacted way?"

- "It is very important that I be able to exercise wherever I travel. It boosts my energy for speeches or coaching engagements. Would it be possible to invite the participants to join me on a morning walk/run and start our session at 9am?"

Boundaries are not about being dogmatic but rather collaborative. If you state what matters and allow others to help you with co-creating solutions, you may find that one exists that you may not have come up with alone.

"I'm just enjoying my life; I suggest you try it." -Tyler Perry

Choose the fish in your fish bowl

Did you ever have parents or a teacher tell you that you must choose your friends wisely. I know so many that listened to this sage advice but didn't truly hear it. In fact, although I desperately should have been given that advice, I probably wouldn't have taken it, because I just love all humans and see good in everyone. I also should have been smacked upside the head many times for being hopeful that the good in some people would eventually shine through.

Truth be told, I don't think I truly realized how important it is to be the curator of your fishbowl until I found profoundly amazing fish to put in mine. I chose my doctors with utmost precision yet didn't really approach my everyday friendships in the same way. Now, I'm not saying I had any bad friends but when you find the right combination of attributes that align with your values and your desired outcomes or even new habits then you've struck gold.

In our case (mine and my hubby, Mike), we both value couples who are passionate toward their love for one another, dedicated to supporting and uplifting one another, who enjoy adventures, have a drive for success and who live very healthy lives. For us, every vacation involves exercise so vacationing with others who do as well keeps us on track to ski hard, bike, walk, scuba dive, snorkel, kayak, do stand-up paddleboard, or play pickleball. We surround ourselves with early risers, avid readers, and lifelong learners. It would be very difficult to get us to move away from these amazing humans.

So, you might be wondering how in the world you choose these fish. Well, it takes trial and error and if there were a friendship-matching app it would sure make it easier, wouldn't it? Ha Ha. Go where they spend their time is what I always say. Find them where you play and exercise. Look for a group to join.

When my husband and I moved to the area we live in, a friend told me to show up to a group bike ride where I would be desperately over my head but where I'd find like-minded people who would drive me to be better because they are insanely strong riders. Well, sure enough, I showed up at 5:30am and was greeted by a kind soul named Riley. He said, "hang on as long as you can and keep coming back and you will eventually keep up with the group". I still laugh thinking about this group.

For a bunch of really smart people, they sure have a funny perception of what an "easy coffee ride" looks like. They claim there are only like 3 hills in the entire ride and I am quite certain there are 7. They have funny math. Well, on that first ride, an incredible woman rode with me and said, "You won't be able to keep up but I want you to come back so I'm going to ride with you and show you the short cuts to be able to find the group and jump on again." Little did I know at the time, but I had just met the glue to many incredible humans who would help me to shape my values and even change my beliefs and actions in life. Nicole and her husband Joe, very quickly embraced our family and introduced us to all of the friendships we treasure to date.

Mike and I were accustomed to moving around but it would take a heck of a lot to uproot us from these absolutely incredible humans who surround us, lift us up, and make us better people.

You see, I had to "show up" to that intimidating group ride to even have this one chance meeting. On that one ride and the coffee that followed, I met people who I would later learn have endured incredible speed bumps in life and triumphed. These are my people.

Every path has its puddle, as the old saying goes.

This is absolutely true in work as well. Aren't we in an age, because of the pandemic, to re-design our lives and our relationships? Well, this is true of the people we choose to work with as well. Really spend time asking questions of the people you plan to work with to find out more about how they spend their time outside of work, what matters most to them, and how they incorporate healthy habits into their lives both inside and outside of work. If you do this and can surround yourself with healthy people, then your new habits will be much more supported. Conversely, if you travel with or work with people who do not understand what you're trying to achieve, then you will eventually be influenced by those actions. If you already have strong healthy habits then those values can be sustained with boundaries - but they won't be appreciated, and sooner or later you'll feel a bit like you are swimming upstream.

"Walk with the wise and become wise; associate with fools and get in trouble" – Proverbs 13:20

Let's just summarize a bit, shall we?

To truly live the most epic and joyful life, you've got to be in control of it. You've got to generate a tremendous amount of happy chemical releases (endorphins) and breath in this great life. If you don't have a great life, then isn't it time to start making it one?

Start by showing up! Show up for yourself, your kids, your friends, your co-workers. Honor your commitments. Do the hard work. Is it easy to show up and eat healthy, cut sugar, and exercise, dance, and laugh every day? Nope. But I've got news for you, this life isn't going to get any easier; you've just got to get tougher.

None of us knows how much life we get on this planet and I, for one, am not going to waste a single day here. As long as I'm not pushing up daisies then I'm going to do epic shit and live an incredible life.

For those who want to ponder and work through some of the brainstorming sessions that I recommended throughout the last couple of chapters, feel free to flip to the last chapter which is the workbook portion.

Thank you for taking the time to read my book and for having an elevated learner mindset. Now get out there and do something epic would you?!

DO EPIC SHIT JOURNAL

These questions are meant to challenge you – take time to discover and explore where they take you. Keep in mind these are the kinds of questions that I often incorporate into coaching sessions and often are accomplished over the course of several months, experiments, and discussions. Often times I begin with an activity that helps you to discover challenges in your life, called a compass. A compass should be visited and reflected on each year as a reset.

Here is an example before you dive into the components that align with this book:

COMPASS

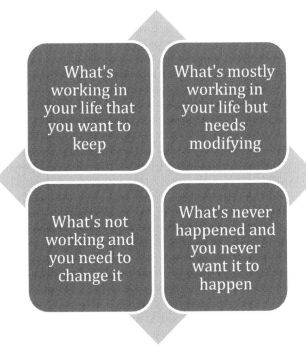

YOUR COMPASS

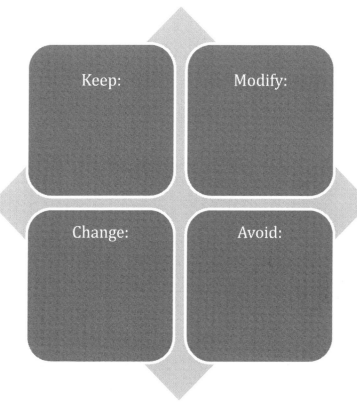

Keep:

Modify:

Change:

Avoid:

CURATE YOUR EPIC LIFE

What does it mean to live an epic life (for you)?

What would it take to live that life?

What are the barriers that exist to achieving it?

CREATE HAPPINESS

What does not bring you joy?

What would it take to cut it from your life?

What would the impact be and can you live with that impact?

Brainstorm: Mini Vacation Moments to Infuse in Your Day

Remember, these are small activities that can shift your energy to something different and enjoyable to break up work or normal schedules in a day.

RANDOM ACTS OF KINDNESS - BRAINSTORMING

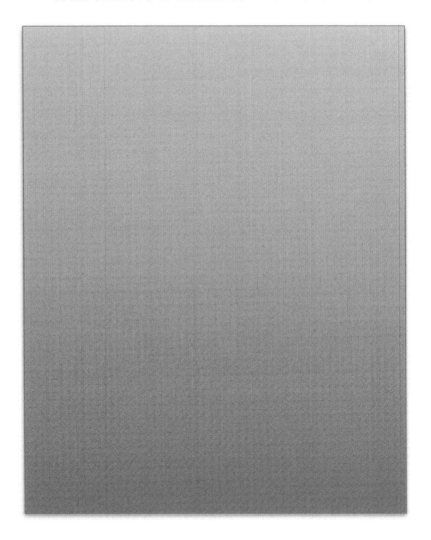

Remember this is about what kind of volunteerism or kindness gestures you could do to uplift the human spirit?

EXERCISE

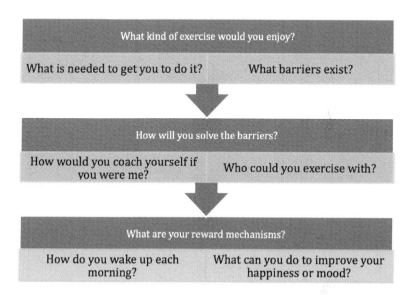

What kind of exercise would you enjoy?

What is needed to get you to do it?   What barriers exist?

How will you solve the barriers?

How would you coach yourself if you were me?   Who could you exercise with?

What are your reward mechanisms?

How do you wake up each morning?   What can you do to improve your happiness or mood?

YOUR RELATIONSHIPS

Who are the fish swimming in your fish bowl?	
What do you value and treasure in the relationships you have on a daily basis?	
What are you missing?	
Where can you make new relationships?	
Are you the kind of friend worth having?	
If not, then what would you need to change in yourself to show up differently for your friends/family?	

Notes:

ACTION PLAN/NEXT STEPS

Action/To Do	Resources	People to	Due

Cheers to your success and happiness and feel free to share with me all of transformations that occur or the challenges you could use some help working on.

You can reach me at victoria@victoriacramer.com or my website is www.victoriacramer.com

Just remember, "Be yourself; everyone else is taken"
– Oscar Wilde

Made in the USA
Middletown, DE
13 January 2023

21959518R00094